A Care for Nature

HENRY B. KANE

A Care for Nature

W · W · NORTON & COMPANY · INC ·

NEW YORK

10397

For my wife Betty
and our children
David, Joanne, and Electa,
fellow observers all,
and active participants
in the affairs of our yard.

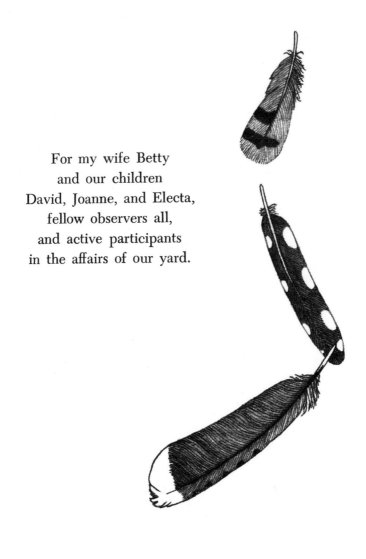

Contents

Illustrations

A Care for Nature

ONE

A Care for Nature

"Before people can become sincerely interested in their environment they must first know what it is, and their education cannot begin too early. As small children they should be given a sympathy for and an understanding of nature." It was a statement made at a large meeting, and the speaker's name is long forgotten. His words, however, are well remembered, for they express, simply and clearly, a precept that has always been basic in our family.

This is the recounting of one family's sympathy for and understanding of nature as it is manifested all about them. It is a recounting of simple things, some of them humorous, some tragic, some beautiful. Most are on a

15

small scale, things that happen in a suburban yard. They are repeated many times every day in other yards all over the country. Yet they are noticed by few, seen with a sympathetic eye by fewer still.

There are those to whom an active interest in nature seems a bootless thing, at least the kind of nature that is all about them. They may travel great distances to view exotic creatures, yet be unmoved by even stranger ones at home. In many instances this is a matter of size. By its sheer bulk a rhinoceros is more impressive than a beetle. Yet there is no such thing as "big" or "small" except in a relative sense. An elephant is big to a mouse, but so is the mouse to a flea. And an elephant is no more than a grain of sand to a mountain. An eye not blind to nature finds beauty and wonder in even the smallest things. Who, on African safari, has seen a creature with ears in its legs? Or one as heavily armored as a tank which can take to the air with ease? Or another which launches into the air on a  parachute and is blown to far places? They are all in our back yard. So are creatures that can lift fifty times their own weight, others that can leap two hundred times the length of their own bodies. We have dead twigs on the cedars that come to life and walk away, and thorns on the bittersweet that not only walk but fly. Where is there beauty to match the flashing color of a hummingbird's throat, the sun-drenched fluttering flight of a tiger-swallowtail butterfly, or the heart-lifting sight of an unbelievably brilliant cardinal flying across a gray winter landscape?

Some years back I came across a book of the early 1890s detailing the adventures of a group of young gentle-men from Boston in the wilds of Maine. Cycling north as far as they could go, when the roads petered out they took to canoes. It was a fascinating story, but it also had its appalling aspects. These were intelligent boys, inter-ested in everything they saw. They were intrigued by the scenery, the trees and flowers, and the wildlife, and they went out of their way to investigate anything new. It was the manner in which they satisfied their curiosity that was the shocker.

At one point the travelers discovered a bulky nest high in a tree, and one of their number climbed up to see if it was in use. He found it to be inhabited by three young hawks, and called the news down below. Some of their number had never before seen young hawks, so the climber lifted the nest from its perch and threw it to the ground. At about that time one of the parent birds returned and circled about screaming piteously, so they shot it down. Bear in mind that these boys were not being maliciously destructive, they were not callously murder-ing wildlife. Their motivation was a sincere interest in nature, and they went about satisfying it in the only way they knew.

Only recently has man begun to take an understanding view of the natural world. He is a vital part of that world, yet since he first rose from the savage state he has consid-ered himself a being apart. He has looked at nature with just one thought in mind—how it could best serve his

interests. Age-old redwood forests have been viewed in terms of board-feet, salt marshes as waste lands to be filled in and "developed," wildlife as inexhaustible sources of income for market hunters and fur traders, and streams as convenient places for depositing refuse. Nature was there to be used by man. That it was more often misused was of no concern. There was so much water and air and land, so many animals on land and fish in the sea, that they could be exploited forever for his benefit.

About the turn of the century a few voices began to be raised against the wanton destruction of nature, but at first they were voices crying in the wilderness. As time went on individuals banded together in groups, but this did little more than make their collective voices louder. To the exploiters, both business and government, they were only irritants, and mild irritants at that. Then, at long last, came a rude awakening. Suddenly it became apparent that his thoughtless despoiling of nature was having an adverse effect on man himself. Concentrations of pesticides and industrial wastes were producing inedible fish; filling of salt marshes was destroying food chains which depleted shellfish supplies; pollution fouled and killed a great lake, making it fit for nothing but surface transportation; belching chimneys and jet-plane and automobile exhausts poisoned the air of big cities and created serious health hazards; detergents seeping into well water made it undrinkable. In many other ways man's unthinking treatment of his environment began to hurt him, and at last those warning voices were heard. "Nature Lovers," viewed with amused tolerance by most of their fellows, suddenly achieved stature as "Ecologists." Politicians and legislators discovered new issues on the side of right. Bills on conservation, anti-pollution, pesticide control, and similar subjects which had died time after time in committee were dusted off and passed enthusiastically. Environmental control took its place as one of the major problems requiring massive and immediate action. There were those who said it was already too late.

How did this situation come about? Why was it allowed to happen? Primarily because of an almost complete lack of knowledge of the natural world and man's place in it. Without comprehension there could be only indifference. Where there was concern it was almost always at the local level: a sportsmen's club becoming incensed because pollution had destroyed fishing in a favored stream; owners of new homes built on filled wetland becoming irate when spring floods poured into their cellars. Not until concerned people put all these individual complaints together did it become apparent that this was a national—in fact, an international—problem of crisis proportions.

At the root of any intelligent action to combat the ills man has brought upon himself must be understanding. How can a doctor treat a patient without a thorough knowledge of the human body, its strengths, and its frailties? How can man restore the natural world to health without thoroughly knowing that world? Public attention is being focused on the problem in many ways. Ballad singers are popularizing ecology songs. The government

has created a folk figure around whom it hopes citizens and action groups will rally. Bands of children and adults, in holiday mood, clean up streams and beaches. Conservation groups produce reams of press releases. In these and other ways the public is being made aware of the problem and its magnitude. But awareness is not understanding. That comes only with a long and continuing interest in and curiosity about the natural world.

Niko Tinbergen, Dutch biologist and noted field observer, writes in his *Curious Naturalists*: "It seems to me that no man need be ashamed of being curious about nature. It could even be argued that this is what he got his brains for, and that no greater insult to nature and to oneself is possible than to be indifferent to nature. There are occupations of decidedly lesser standing."

The ecologist who said that a sympathy and understanding of nature should begin with the very young, did not specify how this should happen. Undoubtedly it is inborn with some. It was with me. But with the vast majority it is something to be learned by example. Shortly after our marriage, my wife and I went to visit friends in the country. When we arrived there was a gorgeous, flaming sunset, a truly breathtaking sight. The young son of the house was playing catch with another lad, throwing a ball back and forth, back and forth. We said, "Oh, Johnny, have you seen that beautiful sunset?" He paused momentarily to look over his shoulder, made an acknowledging comment, "Sunset? Oh, yeah," and then returned to his all-absorbing sport, back and forth, back and forth. We vowed then and there that when our children arrived they would learn to take an active interest in nature from the very beginning. And they did.

It is not enough to teach youngsters an appreciation of nature. It is of vital importance to show a continuing interest in their concerns. How many times we heard our children call, "Mummy, Daddy, come quick and see the sunset," and no matter what we were doing, no matter how busy we were, we rushed to answer that call. After we had quieted their early fears of thunderstorms, we sat on the front steps with them time after time admiring spectacular approaches. A smashing cap of thunder brought happy shrieks, an extra-brilliant flash of lightning drew a series of "Wow!" "Oh, boy!" and other appropriate comments, until finally the drenching rain arrived and drove us indoors.

There were times when the proper reactions placed stern and unusual demands on my wife. She had been taught an unreasoning fear of snakes by her grandmother, so intense that even to come across a drawing of one in a dictionary almost made her faint. Her feelings can be imagined, therefore, when our first-born came into the house one day proudly holding up a little wriggling, squirming garter snake. "Look, Mummy, look what I caught." Rooted to the spot with fear, she nevertheless managed a half smile and said, between clenched teeth, "Yes, dear, it's beautiful. Now don't you think it would be much happier outdoors in the grass?" It was a toss-up whose education was advanced the most by the experience, but I have my own opinion.

Our children are all grown up now. None of them

became natural scientists of any kind, but all have
retained that high regard for nature that we instilled in
them at an early age. They still react appreciatively to
beautiful sunsets, billowing clouds, the first hepaticas of
spring, and fields of daisies. They would no more think of
throwing a candy wrapper out a car window than they
would of dumping old tires in a brook. Anti-pollution and
a kinship with nature go hand in hand. If the woods and
fields and streams are as well loved as one's own home,
there is no more inclination to befoul them than there is
to throw trash on one's living-room floor.

Thoreau, who had a lifelong love affair with nature, had
a word to say about its despoilers. "Most men, it seems to
me, do not care for Nature and would sell their share in
all her beauty, as long as they may live, for a stated
sum—many for a glass of rum." Then, in a remarkable bit
of concern for a distant future, for a menace still a century away, he continued: "Thank God, men cannot as yet
fly, and lay waste the sky as well as the earth! We are safe
on that side for the present." And he concluded this journal entry with a plea that only now is being heeded. "It is
for the very reason that some do not care for those things
that we need to continue to protect all from the vandal-
ism of a few."

To a naturalist there is little new or novel in these
pages. To the vast majority of suburban dwellers, however, they will open unexpected vistas. May their back
yards take on new interest and make them curious about a
world in which there is "no greater insult to nature and
oneself . . . than to be indifferent to nature."

Yard with No Bounds

For the first three years of our married life, my wife and I were apartment dwellers. It must have had certain advantages, I feel sure, although from this distance they are very unclear, especially since we were both country people at heart. Then, in the spring of 1933, we found our three-room apartment in Cambridge getting crowded with guests who had no more liking for it than we did. There were nine spring peepers, a bullfrog, a family of five flying squirrels, and a four-inch tomato worm, a formidable looking creature with a horn on its rear end. It disappeared one day, never to be seen again, and for the

next two weeks my wife carefully turned back the sheets
every night for a detailed inspection.

That was a first-floor apartment, with two windows
facing on a court. On those warm spring nights they were
kept open, and when all ten frogs got going together it
made quite a racket. Probably the only reason our fellow
cliff dwellers never descended on us in their wrath was
that they were unable to locate the source of the disturb-
ance. It was about this time that we decided we deserved
better from life than the anonymity of apartment living,
and in the fall we moved to the country. It was one of
the best decisions we ever made.

The town of Harvard is thirty miles northwest of
Boston. It is apple country, and we lived right in the
middle of an extensive apple orchard. It was beautiful at
all times of the year, but for a week in May it was pure
heaven. Behind us the orchard went on and on to the
edge of a big woods. In front of us was a road, and if
three cars a day went by, that was heavy traffic. Around a
curve to the left lived our landlord. Down the road to
the right, beyond our view, lived his foreman. When the
trees were bare in winter we could see the roof of a neighbor's house across the valley. Up the road a few steps and
through a barway was a pasture whose blueberry bushes,
in season, were heavily laden with fruit. And at the foot
of the pasture, paralleling the road, a little brook mean-
dered between stones and boulders. On occasion it ventured out into small wet meadows and alder swamps, and
if you knew where to look in late fall you could find

clumps of deep-blue bottle gentians. Yes, that was real country.

We lived in Harvard for eight years along with Dixie, a springer spaniel, Mike, our candidate for the world's perfect cat, Mr. Skunk, Mr. Crow, a red-shouldered hawk, and a variety of other pets and temporary guests. Then came the war, and with it, rationing. When tires became unobtainable and gasoline was doled out in minuscule amounts, commuting sixty miles a day became completely unrealistic. So, with heavy hearts, we started house hunting closer to town.

Lincoln was not a haphazard choice. We had visited there, if briefly, and were impressed by its rolling fields, its winding roads, and its extensive wooded areas. It was off the beaten path, with no traffic of consequence through the center of town. As a matter of fact, a stranger passing that way seldom realized he had been through the center of town. Its most distinctive feature was an ancient horse trough standing at the intersection of five roads in front of the library. Furthermore, the commuting distance was cut in half, and I discovered that a number of my confreres at M.I.T. were resident there, making my entry into a driving pool a distinct possibility. It was to these gentlemen that I appealed for help. Frankly, they were not encouraging. Lincoln is a small town. Only rarely do houses become available. When they do, they are snapped up immediately. Then the impossible happened, a phone call that said, "I have just heard of a house near the center of town that was vacated only a few days ago, and . . . " Within minutes we were on our way.

Considering the exigencies of the situation, I suppose we would have taken almost anything habitable, but fortunately we did not have to make a difficult decision. The house itself was undistinguished but not unattractive, a turn-of-the-century structure of two stories plus attic, built on a hillside well above the road. As we walked up the driveway leading to the back yard our eyes were not on the house but on a towering pine tree beside the drive. I think that made up our minds even before we entered the house. We could picture ourselves being lulled to sleep by the wind soughing through its branches, and the wonderful smell of pine being wafted through our windows. To tell the truth we never have heard a single sough, and the nostalgic smell of the north woods has been singularly lacking. I guess it takes more than one tree to do that. In any event, we quickly said yes, and on October 12 we moved in. Thirty years later we are still here, having become owners of our house in the meantime. Now that our place of residence has been established, it is needful to make some explanation of our immediate surroundings, the background against which the events that follow took place.

In late years the word "suburb" has come to mean sprawls of unattractive, jerry-built, boxlike structures crammed close together and stretching off over the horizon. Actually, "suburb" is not a description but a measure of distance, an outlying part of a city. Geographically,

sunken granite posts down by Lincoln Road, and another
pair up back on Tower Road. They mark the limits of that
area to which we hold paper title. But the coons and
skunks, the rabbits and woodchucks, and all the birds that
come to call do not recognize these artificial boundaries.
To them, as to us, ours is a yard that reaches out and back
beyond the limits of vision. It may be stretching the dictionary definition, but neither dictionaries nor granite
markers close us in. Ours is a yard with no bounds.

Somewhere, I suppose, there is recorded a name for our
hill. I have never seen one on any map, nor am I going to
ask at the Town Hall. As far as we are concerned, it is
now, as it has been since we have lived on it, Mrs. Shaw's
Hill. It is topped by a palatial mansion with the greatest
view in town, and since this is a town of hills, there is
plenty of competition. This is where Mrs. Shaw lives, and
I doubt if she has left her hilltop home in years.

The foot of the hill, in our parochial view, lies across
the road in what was formerly woods—"our" woods, we
called them. There were swampy areas where cinnamon
ferns grew waist-high, and they were green with skunk
cabbages and hellebores in spring. A little brook ran
through it, with plenty of stones for building dams, which
our children did with regularity, stones whose removal
disturbed salamanders hiding underneath. There were a
few big pines, in one of which crows nested each year.
There were hillocks crowned by red cedars and carpeted
with running pine, ground pine, and partridgeberries.

There was even an old cellar hole which, in early spring, held its complement of water and spring peepers. A path ran through the woods to the ballfield beyond, a path we shared with cottontails who bounced off at our approach flashing their white powder-puff tails. It was an adventure crossing the brook, leaping from stone to stone, with a misstep meaning wet and muddy shoes.

But now our woods are gone. In their place is a low-slung modern school, surrounded by swings and slides and jungle gyms. There is also a big, circular, hard-topped area whose reason for being we have never discovered. Several times a day hordes of children erupt from the school's doors, to race screaming across hard-packed earth and unyielding black top. I suppose we can be called anti-social, but we much preferred the ground pine and sala-manders and cottontails.

A few feet above our ex-woods is Lincoln Road, two lanes as are all town roads, and one of our principal thor-oughfares. It carries a lot more traffic today than when we arrived. It comes to its eastern end half a mile or so away at the horse trough, and from there roads take off in all directions. You can get almost anywhere from that horse trough. From Lincoln Road a myrtle-covered slope leads up to our lower lawn. I use the term "lawn" loosely throughout, but if our lower lawn in particular leaves something to be desired most of the year, there is no com-plaint in spring when it is purple with tiny violets. About dead center at the top of the slope is a Norway maple, an

ancient tree with a huge spread. In spring and summer its
blossoms and leaves are a real joy. But in autumn, when it
showers down hundreds of thousands of leaves, it
becomes something of a problem. And in spring, when its
progeny push up everywhere in numbers that seem to
increase each year, it is a definite menace. I fail to understand why maples have not taken over the world a long
time ago.

Another slope, where myrtle, jill-over-the-ground.
violets, thyme, and anything else that came to hand are
making progress in killing off the grass (it is a slope too
steep for easy mowing), leads to our small front yard. A
driveway runs up the western side of the yard, with a low
stone wall on its far side and the big pine about halfway
along. The other side of the yard has a row of lilacs, for-

sythia, Japanese quince, and barberry separating us from our nearest neighbor. These shrubs keep a narrow strip in almost permanent shade, ideal for our wild garden. It is planted mostly to ferns, but while they are still in the fiddlehead stage violets flourish, and when the ferns are full-grown their sheltering fronds hide a few wintergreen, pipsissewa, and partridgeberries. For some reason this side did not get terraced and, therefore, slopes down to our garage and the road. At its top, as if intended to separate side and back yards, is a red cedar reaching well above the roof top, and at its foot a great lichen-spotted glacial boulder. It is a magnet for small children who love to climb its sloping side and leap off the other. It was a favorite sport of our children. Now it is of theirs.

Behind the house, at a distance of twenty feet or so, a head-high stone wall fights valiantly to hold the back hill in place. It has been doing this successfully for many years, but there is some question as to how much longer it can keep it up. A wet spring makes the whole hill a fluid mass, and the pressure on the wall is terrific. Its center leans forward now at a precarious angle, and we fear its collapse is imminent. We have thought so for the past ten years.

At the left end of the wall is our pride and joy, the patio. Soon after we became homeowners, my son and I built it in what had been a waste area—a tangle of vines, shrubs, and weeds. It has a brick floor ten or twelve feet square, a shingled roof covering the rear half, and a waist-high stone wall projecting a couple of feet from the retaining wall, whose principal function is to act as a repository for house plants during the summer. Considering the fact that this structure was built of second-hand brick, second-hand lumber, and second-grade shingles, it seems a bit pretentious to call it a patio. But we have yet to find a better name, so patio it is.

When we were digging holes for the cedar posts that hold up the roof, we ran into a concrete slab not much more than a foot down. We discovered that there had once been a barn in this corner cut into the side of the hill. Our patio, therefore, is at the foot of a rather steep if not high slope. We planted it to unusual day lilies and hostas, and topped it with a three-rail cedar fence, the rails having been harvested from "our woods" across the road before the bulldozers got to them. Just above the fence is a row of willows, all of which want to become trees and are, therefore, pruned back regularly. They are not native, I feel sure, for they produce pussies of tremendous size each spring. My tree guide says: "Identifying willows often is a difficult task even for the professional botanist . . . some uncertain specimens may have to be accepted merely as willows." So we accept them merely as willows, and in spite of the fact that their leaves are riddled by insects all summer long, we treasure them as one of the earliest harbingers of spring.

In front of the patio is our garden, four small plots with a bird bath in the middle. Neither my wife nor I is a gardener at heart, and while we want the joy of colorful blooms, we do not want the drudgery of weeding. Some-

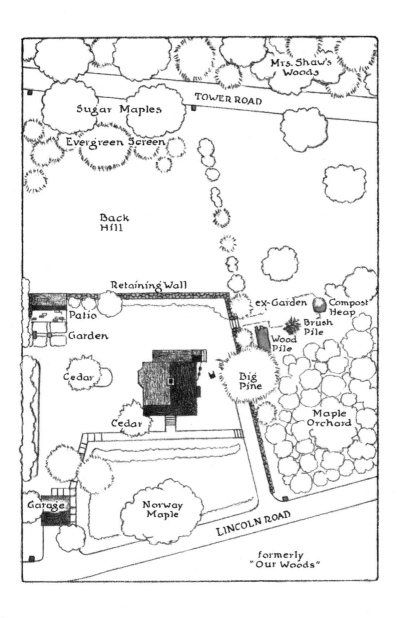

Mrs. Shaw's Woods

TOWER ROAD

Sugar Maples

Evergreen Screen

Back Hill

Retaining Wall

Patio

Garden

Cedar

ex-Garden

Compost Heap

Brush Pile

Wood Pile

Cedar

Big Pine

Maple Orchard

Garage

Norway Maple

LINCOLN ROAD

formerly "Our Woods"

how there are more important things in life. So we sit and admire our little patches of zinnias and marigolds edged with pansies and alyssum, our pots of tuberose begonias, and our boxes of petunias, without the gnawing feeling that there is a big job of weeding to be done and we should be getting at it.

We are essentially isolated on our patio. It is far enough up the hill so that the noise of passing traffic is muted, if not stilled entirely, and there are enough flowers, shrubs, and trees in between to serve as an effective visual screen.

This is rather more space than I had planned to devote to our back-yard retreat. But, as I said, it is our pride and joy, a little island of peace which we share with the bees, the butterflies, and the chipmunks and chickadees who come to partake of the sunflower seeds we strew on the brick floor, or to take them out of our hands. For fifteen years and more it has been such an essential part of our summer living that it could not be passed over casually.

Crowning the back hill is a thick stand of young evergreens—well, maybe teen-agers by now. There are pines, hemlocks, spruces, balsam firs, and a larch that we brought back from Mount Katahdin years ago as a one-inch seedling. It now stands a good eight feet tall. They do just what we expected them to, blank out the traffic on the upper road, and serve as a sanctuary for birds of all kinds. The slope in front we keep open to grass, ferns, milkweed, goldenrod, and patches of moss. This is not accomplished without a fight. If left to itself, that slope would soon be taken over by cedars, oaks, maples, honeysuckle, and on occasion a clutch of poison ivy that somehow manages to sneak in.

Two big sugar maples stand guard at the edge of the upper road, and they are spectacular in autumn. Their branches intermingle with those of oaks across the road, and from there thick woods march on up Mrs. Shaw's Hill. I visited her once, many years ago. Climbing a long, winding driveway through pines, hemlocks, and oaks, I found that the woods ended well below the house. They were not allowed to interfere with the gorgeous view of distant vistas.

Mrs. Shaw, an ardent bird enthusiast of long standing, greeted me warmly when I made known my similar interest. She took me in to see her canaries, dozens of them flying about inside a glass-enclosed room projecting from the rear of the house. They sang and twittered and flew back and forth from one perch to another, with more open space than their kind had seen since they left the Canary Islands. Then we went out to view the feeding area. Against a dense background of evergreens was arrayed the most extensive battery of feeders I had ever seen. No bird would have to wait its turn there. I am sure that the feeders could, with ease, even handle a horde of hungry grosbeaks. This is why I have never been particularly disturbed when any of our feeders runs out of food. The birds know very well where there is plenty more.

There is one other area of our yard that must be described, and in many respects it is the most important of all—the maple orchard. The low stone wall along the far

side of our driveway is broken by four steps leading up
from the back yard to what was once an apple orchard.
After Harvard it hardly warranted that name—a half-
dozen ancient trees which were never sprayed and whose
fruit was, therefore, worthless. But the grass was mowed
each year and it was an attractive open space. On its far
side we could just see our neighbor's roof top and attic
windows. Then the orchard fell into neglect, and it was
immediately taken over by young trees. It was as though
they had been actors standing impatiently in the wings
waiting for their cue to rush on stage, and they did so
with alacrity. The upper part is mostly given over to
oaks and pines, but the lower two thirds has been pre-
empted by maples, thousands and thousands of them, so
thick that they make an almost impenetrable jungle.

A short distance from the top of the steps is our one-
time upper garden. Each year in the optimism of spring
we planted it to an assortment of vegetables, and each fall
we vowed never to do it again. Now the decision has been
taken out of our hands. The sun filters through the leaves
of those young trees only with difficulty. At the far end of
the ex-garden is our compost heap; beside it is a brush
pile much appreciated by small birds and mice; and at
this end a collection of wood of great diversity—old cedar
posts, boards from a torn-down barn, former bean poles,
and fireplace wood from an apple tree that succumbed to
a winter ice storm. Some of this wood has been there so
long that it is returning to the earth from whence it came.

The woodpile provides a welcome home for rabbits, red squirrels, mice, and termites. It is now January, and a woodchuck has been asleep somewhere under there since September.

No doubt there are those who would argue that "yard" is hardly an apt term for the area I have described. Possibly so, but I have no idea where to draw its limits, nor have I any intention of trying to do so. I am in complete accord with our wild neighbors, that if our yard does, indeed, have bounds, they are there only to be disregarded.

THREE

Gourmets and Gluttons

The present popularity of feeding birds is not a custom of long standing. When I was a boy the only recollection I have any kind of bird feeding was after a heavy snow or ice storm. Then the Audubon Society would appeal through the newspapers to the people to throw out bread crumbs to keep the birds from starving. In the early 30s when we moved to the country, none of our friends had feeders, at least as far as I can remember. Today the suburban home which does not boast at least one feeder is rare indeed—and the feederless homeowner is missing a lively subject of conversation at the post office. Widespread feeding of birds is a post-World War II phenomenon.

We put up our first feeder in the mid-30s, and it was only secondarily a feeder. By that time I had become seriously interested in nature photography, and it occurred to me that an ideal way to get close-ups of birds would be to lure them in with food. As a consequence our first feeder was a photographic prop, a short section of an apple limb with a shallow cavity to hold peanut butter and sunflower seeds. The camera and I were hidden in a blind nearby. The arrangement worked well, but when we saw the number and variety of birds it attracted, we became as much interested in watching as photographing and decided it was time we had a proper feeder. These were the depression years, when no one thought of buying anything if he could possibly make an acceptable substitute. Ours was fashioned from a broken apple box and a few pieces of heavier wood retrieved from a tumble-down barn in the neighborhood. It was mounted on an iron rod sunk into the top of a cedar post, had vanes that kept its open side away from the wind, and a piece of glass to close up the back. It was no masterpiece of carpentry, but it has served us long and well. In fact, thirty-five years and several coats of paint later, it is still doing duty as our main feeder.

Before describing some of the interesting things that go on outside our kitchen window, it will probably avoid a bit of confusion if I give a brief account of our setup. We have four feeders, each serving a different purpose. Our principal one, the former apple box, contains sunflower seeds. A suet holder, brought home proudly by our son as his first woodworking project in the fourth or fifth grade, hangs on a corner post of the porch. These are situated directly in front of a kitchen window, the one that is closest to the table. From a wire strung across the outside of the window hangs a peanut-butter log which is made up of a length of red cedar in which I have bored a few holes, and a plastic thistle-seed container, our sole purchase. In addition we spread mixed seed on the ground around the feeder post, and along the top of the wall across the driveway go stale bread, crackers and cereals that have been around too long, and every so often a special treat of dried pumpkin or squash seeds. If we had a more professional attitude, I suppose we would say that, in all, we maintain six feeding stations.

One essential for attracting birds successfully is that there be safe shelters nearby, trees and shrubs to which they can retire quickly in an emergency. We have these in quantity. Our back hill has its thick screen of young evergreens; along the far side of the driveway is the mixed growth—everything from the big pine and cedars to shrubs, the maple forest, and the sizeable brush heap; and hanging over the main feeder are several pine branches that are in constant use by birds both coming and going. The pine branches are only feet away from our bathroom window. Once a guest, who had spent an unconscionable amount of time in the bathroom, emerged at last with the comment, "I don't see how you ever get anyone out of that place. There are so many fascinating things going on outside the window."

The kitchen table is an ideal observation post. In the early morning I sit there with my sketchbook (actually an ordinary pad of paper whose sheets go into the loose-leaf binder later) and record the birds and animals as they put in an appearance. At noon it is my wife's favorite luncheon spot, and on days when the traffic is heavy her soup is apt to be cold before it is finished. The window sill and the edge of the table are invariably lined with young plants and rooting slips, excellent screens through which we peer.

One of the interesting things about watching birds feeding is seeing the difference in their habits. At one extreme are the chickadees, the gourmets; at the other, evening grosbeaks, interested only in how much they are able to put away, greedy gluttons. I have seen seagulls, as a purse seine is being pulled in, gorge themselves with fish to such an extent that they could not lift off the water. I sometimes wonder that grosbeaks do not suffer similarly from overstuffing.

The black-capped chickadee is the state bird of Massachusetts as well as that of our one-time northern province, Maine. I have no idea who was responsible for getting this through a legislature most of whose members probably did not know a chickadee from an English sparrow. I feel sure the Massachusetts Audubon Society played a leading role, but whoever did it could not have

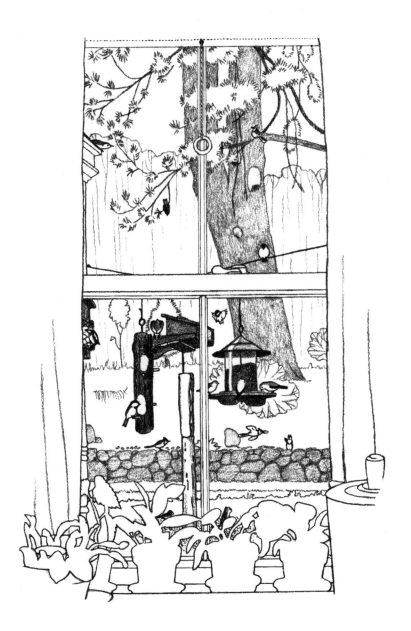

made a better choice. So many of our birds are fair-
weather friends. As soon as the days get shorter and the
nights chillier, they take off for warmer climes and leave
us to fight winter alone. Not so the chickadees. Many
years ago ornithologist Bradford Torey said: "... [the
chickadee is] the most engaging and characteristic enliv-
ener of our winter woods; who revels in snow and ice, and
is never lacking in abundant measures of faith and cheerfulness, enough not only for himself, but for any chance
wayfarer of our own kind."

Not knowing who were the chickadee's backers in the
Great and General Court of Massachusetts, I cannot guess
what arguments they put forth, but they could have done
no better than to quote Walter Prichard Eaton's words,
written fifty years ago in the Berkshires: "... it is doubt-
ful if any of us who dwell in the northeastern section of
the United States ... would yield to any other bird the

first place in our affections held by the little chickadee. Spiritually, he is a tonic that makes for cheerfulness, and there are no standards of value for that."

We enjoy the tonic of our chickadees as they come flitting in to see if we are maintaining the quality of our birds' smorgasbord. They light on the thistle-seed feeder and pick up a few of the little black seeds; then across to the peanut-butter log for a second course; this may be followed by a bit of suet; and a final visit to the main feeder where each one picks up a sunflower seed and flies off to eat it elsewhere. They never try to crowd one another out. If one is in the main feeder the others wait nearby, and as soon as it is vacated a replacement drops down, picks up its seed, and is off again. Most other birds are quarrelsome to some extent, but not the chickadees. They may be impatient, as when a nuthatch spends too much time picking over sunflower seeds and a chickadee lights on one of the feeder vanes as if to urge it on its way. And they have an insatiable curiosity. When we take down the peanut-butter log to bring it in for a refill, they gather around to see what is going on. They balance on the taut wire, cling to the window blinds, and occasionally light on our shoulders or the log itself, meanwhile keeping up a constant inquiring chatter. While we are making all haste indoors to fill the holes, at least one chickadee can be depended on to be peering at us through the kitchen window, and when we go out to rehang the log they descend on it as though they had been starving in its absence.

We rarely see a single chickadee. They come down
from the back hill or across from the maple orchard in
small troops of a dozen or so. One moment there are none
in sight; the next the air is full of them. They never stay
long, maybe five or ten minutes, then they are on their
way. An ornithologist neighbor once made a study of their
travels. He trapped a number of them and decorated them
with red plastic anklets. Then he went around the neighborhood to see what has happening. He found that the
chickadees had a regular route of five back yards, spending no great amount of time in any one. The quality and
quantity of the offerings had nothing to do with their
length of stay. It was simply that these high-strung little
birds always have to be on the go. It is good that this is
so. It would be a sorry situation indeed if Mrs. Shaw's battery of feeders should monopolize their attentions and we
were denied the regular visitations of these confiding
birds that Torrey called "the bird of the merry heart."

Our other most numerous year-round bird is the bluejay, and there is a different personality altogether. Bluejays
are cocky, quarrelsome, impudent, thieving, noisy, and
beautiful. When we first started feeding birds we tried to
drive them away, to reserve our food supply for the small
birds, but we had as much success as Canute with the
incoming tide. There are feeders available today that are
selective, and with a little ingenuity I could no doubt have
made one myself back there in the 30s. Vannevar Bush
did. He had jointed perches surrounding his feeder. They
worked well for small birds, but when a bluejay landed on

one it immediately dropped down and dumped the surprised bird off into space. Not being that inventive, I soon
gave up and, forgetting their bad characteristics, enjoyed
them for their beauty and alertness.

How many times have you ever seen a wild bird leave
the woods and fly directly at you, as if to land on your
shoulder? Probably never. Yet we have that same sensation day after day. As I look out the kitchen window I see
a bluejay in the upper branches of a far oak, or hopping
around the top of an apple tree reaching above the maple
orchard. I see it take off and head directly for me, increasing in size with startling rapidity. I have a fleeting
sensation that it is coming in answer to my unvoiced call.
Then it spreads its wings, opens wide its white-edge tail,
and swoops up to land on the feeder. It is only feet away,
and the feeling persists that it was flying in to me.

Although Thoreau enjoyed most of his wild neighbors

at Walden, he was never greatly taken with jays. "They were manifestly thieves, and I had not much respect for them." He was right, of course, but somehow when I see those brilliant blue birds flashing across a dull winter landscape, when I see them facing courageously into the bitter north wind instead of seeking shelter in the thick branches of an evergreen, I cannot refuse them a certain grudging admiration. In their own ways, chickadees and bluejays add life and hope and beauty to the grayest winter day.

Bird banding has shown that many birds we think of as staying with us all year long are, in reality, migrants, albeit for short distances. The crows, jays, and even some of the chickadees that we see in winter may have spent the summer in New Hampshire or southern Canada, while our summer birds may be down in Connecticut. There is no question at all, however, about most of the others. The first junco is as much a forerunner of winter as the first song sparrow is of spring. This year the date was October 27. I recorded its arrival in my journal:

> This afternoon the first junco appeared. It came directly to the ground under the feeder, although I had not yet put out seed, a situation that was quickly remedied. There seems no question but that this was an old friend who had dined at our table many times before. Why else would it have come to a place where there was no food to attract it? There is plenty of controversy over animal intelligence vs instinct, but there certainly can be

no faulting on memory. I do not know how this gray and
white bird found its way back from Canada or wherever
it had summered. It seems like a very small target for a
trip of even a relatively short distance. But however it
was accomplished, there is no doubt that it had a very
definite destination in mind. I do hope its memory of our
varied fare lives up to expectation.

That first junco did not have long to wait before it was
joined by others of its kind as well as tree sparrows and a
few white-throated sparrows. They are all ground feeders,
and seem well pleased with the Mixed Wild Bird Feed,
which has become a staple in stores everywhere. By and
large they feed peacefully together. If there are sudden
flare-ups, it is invariably between birds of the same kind,
a junco senior citizen asserting its authority over an
upstart youngster. But there is no real enmity involved,
and after a momentary retreat, the young bird is right
back again.

There are other ground feeders. Mourning doves are
regular visitors, one or two at a time. They are dressed in
modest Quaker gray and tend strictly to business. However, they are not to be put upon with impunity. One day
as I sat at the table making quick sketches of a dove from
many angles, a pair of bluejays flew in. One stopped off at
the feed tray, the other landed on the ground. The small
birds immediately fled, but the mourning dove paid no
attention. Evidently one of the jays felt its mastery ques-
tioned, for it hopped toward the dove with the obvious

intent of driving it off too. That was a mistake. The peaceful gray bird turned quickly and went for the jay. Taken completely by surprise, the attacker leaped backward into the air and hurried away. A moment later the second jay dropped down to continue the harassment, and met with the same response. Beneath that mild Quaker exterior beat a heart that could be filled with righteous wrath when the occasion demanded.

There are also a pair of cardinals with their thick red beaks (they belong to the grosbeak family), their martial crests, and the male's startling coat of brilliant scarlet. Cardinals and tufted titmice are southern birds who have gradually worked their way north. In the 20s, Forbush called the cardinal a rare visitor to New England. In the 30s, Peterson set the northern limit of its range in the east as southern New York. Ludlow Griscom, writing of the birds of our immediate area in 1949, called it a "rare vagrant," and gave only one authentic sighting, that in 1905. Two years ago, whenever we saw either a cardinal or a titmouse, it was the occasion for a minor celebration. Now the titmouse pair come in several times a day, the two cardinals at less frequent intervals, maybe every other day on the average. Last summer both pairs brought in their offspring on several occasions, all of whom have since left for parts unknown. It is suspected that the abundance of bird feeders is responsible for this northward trek. They were unable to sustain themselves in winter on the natural food supply, but with this help they are doing very well indeed.

As for the pest birds, starlings, English sparrows, and pigeons, we are grateful for the fact that they bother us very little. I only remember seeing one pigeon, and it stayed for just a few minutes. They probably do so well at the battery of feeders atop the hill that they see no need to look elsewhere. Our visiting nurse said one day in a shocked voice, "Do you know you have a neighbor who actually feeds pigeons?" I did. Many a time I have seen them going to or coming from the sumptuous spread on the hill.

The other two pests have never been a great problem because they frighten so easily. I shall never understand why two birds who are so adjusted to humans in the city become wilder than native birds when they go feral and move to the country. If an English sparrow is feeding with mixed company on the ground, simply appearing at the window is enough to send it flying off, while the other birds pay no attention. However, we are not in the least concerned about the "why" as long as the desired result is achieved.

Pheasants seem to be able to take us or leave us, and this is a leave year. Not a one has come in so far. We see them frequently, but they probably prefer the hilltop feast of plenty. Yesterday two cocks came racing down from there as though they were running an Olympic dash, probably full of cracked-corn energy. Some winters we have had them off and on, but never with any regularity. When they do come in their table manners are perfect, but this is only to be expected. With their overpowering size it would be undignified to pay any attention to their small fellow boarders.

One thing that has always interested us is the ease with which pheasants dig through new snow cover to the seed layer hidden below. They are excellent snow shovelers. Sometimes they scratch with their feet like barnyard fowls, but they also use their strong beaks. With quick side-to-side sweeps they send the snow flying, and in no time at all they have reached the seed level. It is rather like sweeping off the front walk after a fall of light snow and discovering a layer of frozen foods hidden below.

Our original thought in putting out bread crusts on the stone wall was that it would keep the jays away from the feeders. That was a forlorn hope. For one thing there was never enough bread to keep them busy for long. As soon

as a new supply was spread out they descended in droves and carted it off. It disappeared like snow before a spring rain. Only rarely does a jay eat there on the wall. The idea seems to be to make off with the most food in the shortest time. After a brief inspection, presumably looking for the largest piece, the jay flies off with it, hides it, and quickly returns. I have seen where some of these treasures are hidden, and I wonder how many are ever recovered. They get tucked under clumps of grass and dead leaves, or poked into cavities in trees and in crotches of their branches. Surely mice and squirrels get the benefit of most of them.

I feel certain the downy woodpeckers consider they have a proprietary interest in the suet feeder. To be sure, chickadees and nuthatches visit it quite often, but the downys are its most frequent customers. They make very cautious approaches, landing overhead on a vertical pine branch first, then hitching up and down, often for minutes, while keeping an eye on the suet. When at last a downy is satisfied that the coast is clear, it flips down and hammers away with a noise that is heard all through the house. Every now and then its look-alike big brother, the hairy woodpecker, shows up. A hairy is not really large, about the size of a robin, but it is so much bigger than the downys that it seems to be the size of a crow. On occasion a red squirrel or a marauding starling attacks the suet with the intention of making off with the whole piece. And once in a while it succeeds.

Just as the suet feeder belongs to the downys, so the

peanut-butter log is chickadee country. For years there was a common belief that undiluted peanut butter was too cloying for birds to take, that it was apt to be fatal, in fact. We used to go to great pains mixing in corn meal, oatmeal, or bird seed. I guess they enjoyed it all right, although the chickadees seemed to pick out the seeds and throw them away, a difficult job when they were all stuck together with peanut butter. Now, however, our local Audubon people say there is no truth in the rumor, so today's chickadees take their peanut butter straight, just as we do.

Until very recently thistle seeds were unknown as an article of commerce. Because Lincoln is a hotbed of bird lovers, they arrived here early and were an immediate success. On the bag was the promise that they would "attract goldfinches and pine siskins," so we were among the early purchasers. We had never seen any pine siskins but they sounded exotic, like something we ought to have if we were to hold up our heads among our peers.

For the first year or more our thistle seeds brought in only goldfinches, but that was reward enough. We could watch the season changes in the males' coloring, from drab yellow-green to brilliant gold. I had always thought that this was accomplished by molting, but the experts say no, that the gold feathers are there all the time, hidden by dull colored tips. In due course the tips wear off, and the bright coloring is exposed. I have never quite understood how a bird gets much wear on the middle of

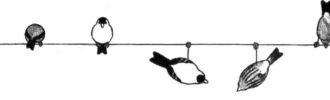

its back, but I guess those experts would have an answer, if I ever bothered to ask.

We had just about given up on the siskins when one day a goldfinch showed up that did not look quite right, somehow. I rushed for the bird book and sure enough, we had our first pine siskin. Frankly, it was something of a disappointment. A little smaller than a goldfinch but with the identical shape, it had the coloring of an undistinguished sparrow. There was certainly nothing exotic about its appearance. However, there was no question about its pugnacity. When that first one was followed by others of its tribe, the goldfinches were quickly dispossessed.

Our thistle-seed feeder is a plastic cylinder with a conical cover and a trough at the bottom, surrounded by a circular perch. No more than four birds are allowed on the perch at one time, and when a flock of fifty or so arrive at once, there are a dozen birds trying to oust each of the lucky four. They gather on the wire overhead, on the feeder wire, and on the nearby peanut-butter log. I have filled pages with sketches of some of the improbable positions they get into. And with regularity they make sorties on the four incumbents. Sometimes a siskin succeeds, but I have yet to see a goldfinch do so. Pine siskins live in the far north, as far north as Ungava and the mouth of the

Mackenzie, and probably up there they have to battle for every last seed in order to survive. In any event, they are natural-born fighters. The goldfinches must be greatly relieved when they see the last of them in the spring.

With all the activity elsewhere, however, the main feeder, the old apple box with its pile of sunflower seeds, is where the real action is. There was, for example, the morning a family of jays used it as a base for some sort of bluejay game they were playing:

October 7: For a time this morning our bluejay family was playing its own version of musical chairs. At least I assume it's the pair and their second crop of young. There were six or seven of them altogether, and they definitely seemed to be playing a game. One would swoop down to the feeder and displace its occupant who would then fly up and take over a perch from another jay who, in turn, would flip across and change places with a third jay, and so on and on. The air was filled with flashes of blue, in and out, up and down. None of them was angry, none was asserting authority. It was, quite obviously, all in the name of sport, and it certainly livened up a gray, foggy morning.

As an aerial display, though, the bluejay family's could not compare with the May Day dance we were treated to one year. Early in the morning we had a number of arrivals. There were mourning doves, pine siskins, goldfinches, tufted titmice, chickadees, nuthatches, bluejays, downy

woodpeckers, and purple finches. Altogether it was quite
a collection.

Then, in mid-morning, a flock of a dozen or more evening grosbeaks arrived, and many of the others were still
there. The air was full of birds, landing on feeders, on
the ground, flying up into the pine branches, exploding
into the air all at once at some fancied danger, then fluttering down again like a flight of brilliant butterflies. The
yellow of the grosbeaks and goldfinches, the blue of the
jays, and the purple-red of the finches, all these made a
breath-taking display of flashing color. This was a May
Day spectacular without equal.

Which brings us to the gluttons, the evening grosbeaks.
Like the cardinals and titmice, these are birds that have
extended their range into New England during this century. Originally they were native to the far northwest, but
during the 1800s they worked their way across the country. The males are strikingly colored in black, white, and
gold, the females more subdued but still handsome. They
travel in flocks of up to a hundred, and where sunflower
seeds are plentiful they may stay for a long time. We have
never had any really sizeable flocks, usually one or two
dozen at a time.

First they light in the pine tree, then they come in to the
feeder or the ground beneath it. Some flutter down and
hover at the feed tray like out-sized hummingbirds.

Others plummet to the ground and make crash landings. They are not overly quarrelsome, although every now and then a couple will engage in a brief flyup. Their only real interest, though, is in eating. Everything else is subordinate to that. Sometimes they all go up and sit in the pine tree for short periods, probably too stuffed with seeds to move. However, a bird's digestive juices work fast, and before long one bird returns to the festive board, then another, and soon all are back. And when our supply is exhausted, off they go to that never failing supply at the top of the hill.

Anyone who tries to satisfy the insatiable appetites of evening grosbeaks has started on the road to bankruptcy. I have one wish, which I know will never be fulfilled, that they would spend a part of their time gobbling down some of their natural food supply which includes maple seeds. A flock of a hundred or so, working over our yard, would save me many back breaking hours of pulling up young maple trees, hundreds of them every year. It seems little enough to ask in return for our bounty.

FOUR

The Crazy Season

Spring is that time of the year when the earth is released
from the icy clutch of winter, when the sun climbs higher
and shines longer, when warm breezes open up buds
which have waited long months through ice and snow
and sleet and freezing rain. It is the season most dear to
the hearts of poets, young lovers, and compulsive garden-
ers. It is also the season when animals do the craziest
things. Consider, for example, the Ballet of the Compost
Heap.

We had never thought of our bulging pile of last year's
leaves as a stage for any kind of performance, let alone a
ballet. When we discovered it did, indeed, serve such a

61

purpose, it came as a complete and fascinating surprise. At first we were mystified. Two flickers stood facing one another, their necks extended to the limit, their bills pointing at the sky like a pair of half-sized bitterns trying to look like dead cattails in a swamp. Then they began to bob and nod. Up and down, down and up went their heads, as though keeping time to some rhythmic beat all their own. It seemed as though they should be doing a soft-shoe shuffle to make the dance complete.

Over and over the awkward, jerky movements were repeated. Then came time for intermission, or maybe it was the end of a sequence. The two birds wandered away, not very far to be sure, but pointedly paying no attention to one another. At length, as though an invisible prompter had given an unheard signal, they rushed back to the compost heap and once again went into their formal ritual. The courting or the mating dance of the flicker? It could be either one, according to Forbush. Edwin Way Teale watched such a display for some time, two males vying for the affections of a female who seemed singularly unimpressed. While they were doing their best to gain her favor, she was wandering about foraging through the dead leaves.

In any event, it is a ludicrous performance, made doubly so by the earnestness of the participants. To them there is nothing funny about this bobbing and weaving and neck-stretching. It is a serious business. As a matter of fact, considered as a dance form, it is rather stately compared to some that humans have dreamed up. But

since no one has yet done a bugaloo or a frug on our compost heap, we shall have to call the dance of the flickers
our silliest terpsichorean exhibition to date. As I say, there
has been little competition.

In point of fact, our yard sees more fighting than dancing in the spring. This is the time when a male bird is
being called upon constantly to defend his territory or
maybe just assert his dominance. Our house robin gets
into scraps on occasion when another male fails to move
through his home grounds fast enough to suit him. For a
while the two seem to think they are game cocks, ruffling
out their feathers and flying up at one another. Actually it
is a rather half-hearted performance, more of a formality
than anything else, to prove that they are, indeed, cock
robins. It seldom lasts long, and the interloper flies off
when he tires of the whole thing.

Much more in earnest are the wild chases in which
robins engage at this time of year. Suddenly, without
warning, two birds come streaking around a corner of the
house. They are only inches apart like a pair of jet fliers
doing daredevil close-formation aerobatics. At top speed
they dodge recklessly in and out around trees and bushes.
They swoop down almost to the ground, then swirl up
over the roof top, only to appear again from around the
front of the house and flash through the narrow opening
between the lilacs and the willows. They travel so fast
that it is impossible to distinguish their sex. As Arthur
Cleveland Ben says, " . . . we are left in doubt whether the
pursuits are amatory or hostile."

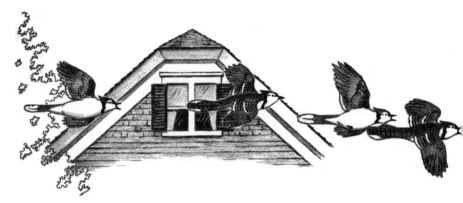

Less spectacular but much noisier are the spring pursuits of bluejays. One morning as I left the front door to go down to the driveway for our paper, a mob of screaming jays swept low overhead. There were six or eight of them strung out in a ragged line. They had hardly disappeared from sight before they were back again, just as noisy as before. They went off in the same direction from which they had come. Was this an amatory chase, a bunch of gentlemen jays pressing their loud suit on a popular lady? Was it a close-knit family driving off an unwelcome interloper? Or was it just vernal exuberance? Jays abhor silence, except during the nest-robbing season, and it is highly probable that this was nothing more nor less than a bit of group exhibitionism or possibly a follow-the-leader kind of game. Whatever the cause, they were certainly enjoying themselves.

Our backyard chases are not solely an avian phenomenon. One of the earliest signs of a spring still to come is the breakneck performance of red squirrels racing through the trees. They spiral up and down the big pine

at such terrific speed that it seems impossible their feet can be touching the rough bark. The ascent seems no slower than the downward dash. They tear out along limbs and leap unbelievable distances to other trees. There is no question about the motivation here. It is definitely amatory. But this is a mated pair who live together in the big hole in the pine. So these lightninglike chases are probably the fulfillment of an age-old urge, an essential part of the welcome to spring, the squirrel equivalent of a Maypole dance.

If the robins' battles lack enthusiasm, the same cannot be said of pheasants' cockfights. All through one winter, three of these stately birds had visited us on occasion, two striking cocks and a hen. Sometimes they came to see what largesse we had provided for our ground-feeding birds. At other times they merely wandered up through the deep snow of the maple orchard on the way to the more lavish spread they knew was waiting at the top of the hill. The larger of the two cocks and the hen were probably a pair, and we assumed the third was an offspring of the previous year. He was not only smaller in size but he had no distinguishable "ears," a notable characteristic of the supposed patriarch.

On a morning in spring the young cock was poking about under the feeder, peacefully picking up an early breakfast. Suddenly there came a raucous crowing, and I looked up to see the old cock pheasant on top of the compost heap at the end of the upper garden. He was settling his feathers back into place after that strenuous effort, and just then he spotted the younger bird. Without a moment's hesitation he came racing across. Through the dead grass and weeds, down the slope and over the stone wall, across the driveway and up the near slope, he came at breakneck speed. The younger bird saw the attack coming, but made no effort to escape. Instead he met his challenger face to face.

Then began the battle, as impressive a fight as any two game cocks ever put on. Time after time they flew up at one another, beaks agape, feathers ruffled out so that they seemed twice normal size, long tails streaming out behind. The battle moved away from the feeder into the driveway, and gradually down onto the lower lawn. It seemed as though the old bird was forcing the younger back and back, but in the mix-up it was really impossible to tell one from the other. Although they were near the road, it was early in the morning and no cars went by to disturb their set-to. Probably the whole thing lasted ten or fifteen minutes, or maybe it only seemed that long. I was too engrossed to keep time, but at last they gave up, and the battle came to a unique and unexpected conclusion. Both birds squatted down facing one another, their necks stretched out on the grass, their heads only inches apart. For long minutes they remained in that position. Was it just the end of Round 1? Were they regaining their energies for a second go? After the heat of that lengthy encounter it seemed a logical assumption. But logic, at least my logic, had nothing to do with it. At last they got to their feet, shook their feathers back into position, and side by side stalked across the driveway and off through the maple orchard. As they disappeared in the thick tangle they were pecking for food as unconcernedly as they had all winter long. It had been no real battle after all, only a tourney, father and son engaging in mock combat, apparently asserting their masculinity in the hot-bloodedness of spring. Serious or not, it was a confrontation to be remembered.

If a sham battle appears to be normal springtime behavior, there are other performances which are not. How can this be explained?

It was an early morning in late March. I looked out the window to see a cock pheasant tearing uphill just beyond the pine tree. He disappeared behind the woodpile, and it was several minutes before he reappeared at the other end, sauntering along slowly and sedately. Then, suddenly, he turned right and dashed full out across the length of the garden. He came to a stop just above the old

apple tree, then for two or three minutes walked casually about, in no hurry to go anywhere. At last, lowering his head and raising his tail so they were in a straight line, he dashed madly down through the maple orchard at full tilt.

There were no other pheasants in evidence. He was not showing off before a lady or chasing a real or fancied rival. It was possible, of course, that he had eaten something that did not agree with him, like Gilbert and Sullivan's dickey bird, but I rather suspect it was just another manifestation of the madness of spring.

It must not be thought that all our wild neighbors react to spring with such unseemly actions. There are also moments of tenderness and affection, moments that seem to require no involved analysis or speculation as to their intent. There was, for example, what we called in our relations to neighbors, "The Case of the Kissing Cardinals." It happened on a morning in March. Spring was only four days old. I glanced at the feeder just in time to see the male cardinal leaving. He flew into the low blueberry bush under the pine tree, and there the female was waiting. He was not carrying a sunflower seed in his bright red beak, not bringing her an offering of food. But he landed right in front of her, reached out and kissed her! At least they touched beaks, and if that is not kissing I know no better word for it. Then they flew off together.

An even more convincing example of what we consider an essentially human action occurred one year in late

winter. I watched a thirsty pine siskin having the day's
first drink in the pine tree. A small mound of snow sat on
top of a thick mass of pine needles, and the siskin sat on
top of it, pecking away at the chilly crystals, real ice
water. Soon another siskin landed nearby, and judging
from subsequent actions, a bird of the opposite sex.
Undoubtedly siskins can tell that sort of thing, although
to me they all look exactly the same. In any event, the
first bird immediately stopped drinking and hopped
across to the twig where the newcomer perched. Then
came the display of amour. He (she) reached out and
touched bills with her (him) gently, briefly. It was
repeated again and again, maybe a couple of dozen times.
The end came when another siskin landed nearby, and
one of the love-makers immediately flew over to greet it.
Was it an unfaithful male or a fickle female? Whichever it

was, the call to breakfast seemed to be a greater urge, for
in a moment all three flew down to the thistle feeder.
Would that all such triangles could be settled as easily!

The Crazy Season of spring is full of surprises. It is a
time of combat, mad pursuit, strutting displays, and
tender advances. The only thing predictable about our
wild back-yard neighbors is their unpredictability.

FIVE

Trapped!

Even before he had completed his Walden retreat, Thoreau discovered that he was to have company. "The mice which haunted my house were not the common ones ... but a wild native kind not found in the village." He was not able to identify them, but he was impressed by their friendliness and complete absence of fear. We also have this "wild native kind" as fellow inhabitants in winter, as does everyone who lives in the country or outer suburbs. They are whitefooted mice, nocturnal creatures with reddish brown backs and white underparts, big ears, and black shoebutton eyes. (There is a word that dates one!) My wife, who is no mouse enthusiast, holding one in the palm of her hand for the first time, said: "Why he's beautiful. He doesn't even look like a mouse."

Unfortunately, beautiful and friendly as they are, white-

73

feet in one's house are also a nuisance. One year we discovered a sizeable piece chewed out of a favorite table-
cloth stored in the linen drawer; before we dare to put on
our boots and overshoes which are lying in the back hall,
they are always shaken out to empty them of sunflower
seeds; and these restless and agile creatures keep us awake
at night scurrying back and forth through the partitions.
So they have to be trapped out.

Thirty years ago we had thirteen whitefeet in a cage at
one time, an adult pair who had produced two families in
quick succession. They posed obligingly for countless
photographs, so many and so varied that a book was inev-
itable. That was the first of a series of six life histories
under the general title of *Wild World Tales*; and these
were followed by three more in a habitat series: the life of
a pond; a meadow; and a wood. They have done reasonably well, and we are eternally grateful to the whitefooted
mice who started it all.

We set our live trap in a pantry cupboard, baited with
peanut butter and sunflower seeds, and tend it regularly
each morning. When a mouse is caught we first apologize
to it for the inconvenience, then transport it as soon as
possible to South Lincoln, a mile away, and let it go at the
edge of a wood, in a spot directly opposite a church. We
figure that gives it a rather broad choice: either to go
back to the woods or to take up an ecclesiastical life. We
have not heard that the church is overrun with mice, but
then, we have never asked.

Dorothy Lathrop, one of America's foremost writers

and illustrators of children's books, also produced a book
about whitefooted mice, *The Littlest Mouse*. She lives in
the country in northwest Connecticut, and one winter I
had a letter saying, "I get my exercise walking down the
road a safe distance to let our trapped whitefeet loose."
No one who has ever had close contact with these confiding little creatures could ever think of using a killer trap,
most especially if they are owed a debt of gratitude for
helping bolster the family income. It would be a sorry
way to repay a debt.

Most of our wild guests are welcome. They offer us
unlimited entertainment and ask little in return—a snack
at the feed tray, a nectar-gathering visit to the garden, a
nesting site in a tree, a home under the woodpile,
rights to pine-cone and cedar-berry gathering. These are
things to which they have a natural claim, and we are
pleased to have them exercise it. Gray squirrels, however,
are not on our welcome list. If given a chance, they dis-
possess the red squirrels from their pine-tree home. They
have no trouble climbing over the metal guard on the
feeder post, and they sit there in the feeder stuffing themselves until every last sunflower seed has gone. Furthermore, I cannot get over the oft-repeated description of
them as "nothing but bushy-tailed rats." The simple fact is
that we do not like gray squirrels, and we trap them out
with alacrity and great satisfaction.

When the bird-feeding season starts in the fall, the
Havahart live trap comes out of storage along with the
feeders. We do not leave it permanently set, but it is

always nearby on the back porch, and at the cry, "Here comes a gray," it is rushed into duty. Before we got that trap we tried time after time to frighten the grays. The first attempt, rushing out on the porch with waving arms and Comanche yells, sent the culprit fleeing high up the cedar by the path to the upper garden. It might take it as long as half an hour to return. The second was a repeat of the first, but accompanied by throwing some of the smaller pieces of firewood stacked on the porch. This time the villain would go as far as the pine tree and peer out from behind it. Retrieving the wood later, especially in a time of deep snow, was an unwelcome chore. The interval before return was much shorter the second time. And the third attempt was invariably a complete failure. Having decided our yells were harmless and our firewood exhausted, the retreat now went only halfway to the pine, and the bushy-tailed miscreant stood there looking back insolently over its shoulder. That insolent look was another reason for our dislike. This time, as we were going back inside the house, the gray was already return-ing to the feast. So then we got our Havahart, squirrel-size.

Live trapping can become something of a game, full of uncertainties and suspense. It is with us. Once a gray came across the driveway, up over the slope, and walked directly into the trap. It never happened that way again. Usually the sequence goes something like this. A squirrel comes down the pine and advances confidently to the feeding ground. In anticipation I have arranged a fine display of sunflower seeds around the mouth of the trap and inside its gaping maw. We stand in the kitchen watching the approach of our intended victim. There is no time wasted in discovering the concentration of food, and the gray settles down to enjoy its feast. At intervals it reaches inside the trap, then, while we cheer it on with, "Go ahead, go in, farther, farther . . . ," it backs out again and hops off out of sight around the corner of the house. We groan in frustration, but minutes later it returns and our hopes rise once more. This time the grass gets thoroughly searched, the squirrel rooting through it like a pig. When it heads back to the trap at last, as like as not it will climb up on top. Surprisingly, the trap is rarely sprung by this maneuver. Then there may come a period of tunneling underneath, digging out the seeds that have fallen through the openwork floor. And so back to the mouth of the trap again, a circuitous return. Once more we hold our breath as the squirrel repeats its previous performance, advancing into the trap, retreating, advancing a bit farther the next time, until at last it nudges the treadle and

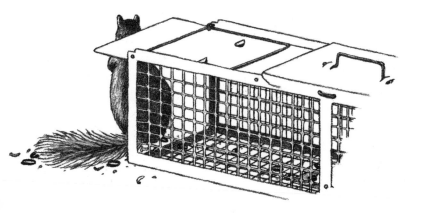

the door clangs shut behind it. We breathe again and rush out to make sure it is closed tight. The suspense is over.

The squirrels do not enjoy their enforced incarceration. They charge back and forth, try to gnow through the heavy wire, gnash their teeth, and snarl when we come near. I have read that rodents have a compulsive feeding instinct when they are injured or in danger, and these squirrels certainly bear that out. They invariably clean out the peanut butter on the treadle in short order. We try not to keep them any longer than possible and release them in a congenial spot, far removed from our yard. The cemetery is the usual loosing ground. It has a fine growth of oak trees, and plenty of other squirrels for company. We hope they find it to their liking and will not be tempted to make a return trip.

If we are something less than enthusiastic about our gray squirrels, the same cannot be said about the reds. We enjoy them thoroughly, and have done so ever since they took up residence in the pine tree twenty or more years ago. Their alertness, their headlong flight through the trees, their appealing posture as they sit up with front paws folded over their chests, tail curved up over their backs, and a look of wonder in their sparkling eyes—these things endear them to us. We do shoo them out of the feeder on those occasions when snow weighs down the overhanging pine branches and makes it easy for them to leap down. And we realize full well that if they ever get into the house they can be very destructive. So far we have been spared any house incursions, but there was one amazing happening that came all too close.

November 14: We may have to change our minds about the red squirrels being our friends, in fact I guess we already have. There have been no resident reds since last winter's occupant of the pine tree hole was run over right at the foot of our driveway. Recently, however, another one has put in an appearance. It is small, probably a young of the year, and not living in the tree but in the woodpile. At any rate, it has discovered our ground feed and also how to get onto the roof by way of the cedar at the corner of the front porch. I may have heard it in the attic, but I am not sure of that and I certainly hope I am wrong. Today, though, it has been up to something new, and this is the end of an incipent friendship. First I heard a thumping on the front porch, as though someone was knocking gently on the storm windows. There was no one there, so I went upstairs and looked out on the porch roof. There was the young red squirrel lifting corners of asphalt shingles and letting them thump back into place. I thought it was after maple seeds caught under the edges—there were plenty of them. But later on the same noise came from the roof over the stair landing, and I got a closer look at what was going on from the bathroom window, no more than three or four feet away. To my amazement the little devil was breaking off corners of the shingles, then sitting up and nibbling on the asphalt chunks. I cannot imagine what sort of craving this satisfies, but maybe it makes as much sense as some things young humans eat, not to mention smoke and sniff. However, when red squirrels take to eating the roof off over our heads, literally, a beautiful and long-enduring friendship has come to an end. This one, at least, will have to go.

November 15: Our roof destroyer has gone. This afternoon it walked into the trap, and in short order had
taken up residence in the cemetery. There it will find
plenty of company, if only with other Kane squirrels, but
it will certainly have to develop new appetites.

So ended our first real falling out with any of the red
squirrels we had come to regard as friends. We hope it
will be the last.

There was also a time when another member of the
order Rodentia incurred our wrath. Each spring we plant
six tomato plants along the back of the house. They get
the sun's heat in front and also in back, reflected from the
clapboarding, and they do very well. Usually we settle on
one variety, Big Boy, Marglobe, or something else that
has been highly recommended, but one year we went
experimental. We put in one each of six different varieties.
I do not remember now which one it was, maybe the
Early Hybrid, but one of them produced a huge tomato.
With great interest we watched it outstrip all the others,
and we could hardly wait for it to ripen fully so we could
find out if it was as tasty as it was magnificent. Then trag-
edy struck. One day we found that something had eaten a
piece out of the top of our splendid specimen. Who was the
culprit? From the position of the hole we suspected a
bird of some sort, maybe a bluejay. It was too high to
have been made by a rabbit, and a coon would have
simply pulled it down, probably plant and all. Later, as
we sat out on the patio, the mystery was solved. Around
the corner of the back porch came a chipmunk. It skipped

lightly over to the tomatoes, climbed nimbly to our vio-
lated prize, and settled down to lunch. That did it. Out
from storage came the Havahart.

We set the trap right in front of the tomatoes, thinking
it would reduce our chances of catching an innocent chipmunk, some of whom were very friendly. It took almost
no time to catch the offender. We had hardly retired to
the patio, a discreet distance away, when it came bounc-
ing across the grass, went right into the trap, and the door
swung shut behind it. We were elated. Our tomato was
gone, but it had been sacrificed for the well-being of its
fellows. Now they were safe. We made the familiar trip to
the cemetery and returned with a satisfied "mission
accomplished" feeling. A short while later I went out the
back door, and as I rounded the corner a chipmunk
leaped down from the top of our mutilated tomato! That
did it. Then and there war was declared. It came to an
end seven chipmunks later.

As with the chipmunks, we did not always make the
right catch on the first attempt. Time after time, when the
trap was set under the feeder for a gray squirrel, I had to
go out and release an inquisitive chickadee or junco. One
day during the migration season a purple grackle came
strutting across the lawn. We were intrigued to see that it
was wearing an anklet. Someone, somewhere, had been
banding grackles. As we had never before had occasion to
report a band, we hoped it would get caught, and sure
enough it did. I wondered to whom we would report it,
but there on the band was complete information,

"963-22089. Write F. & W. Serv., Wash. D. C." I would probably have had trouble reading that on a humming-bird band, but on this grackle-sized one it was readily legible even without a magnifying glass. We immediately sent our report to the F. & W. Serv., then waited impatiently for a reply.

I suppose thousands upon thousands of band returns come in every year, and it must be a time-consuming process to answer each one (to both finder and bander) in enough detail to make it meaningful. We caught the grackle on October 20. A few weeks later we had an acknowledgment and a request for further information, but otherwise we heard nothing all winter. Of course it was just plain curiosity on our part, and it did not make

the slightest difference how soon it was satisfied. These
birds breed as far north as New England and winter along
the Gulf Coast from Florida to Louisiana. We wondered
if it had been banded in the rice fields last winter, or
maybe in the Virginia hills on its way north in the spring
Our speculations came to an end the following April
when we had a reply. "Records . . . indicate that this band
was placed on a bronzed grackle near South Lincoln,
Mass., on 7/19/69." That was only a month before we
caught it, and only a mile or two from here. Well, I guess
not every report can be expected to set a new record or
even bring word from distant parts. I was also a bit dis-
mayed to hear that our purple grackle had been identified
by someone else, probably much more knowledgeable, as
a bronzed grackle, until I looked them up. Peterson says
that the experts are not at all agreed that they are separate species, that "some of us believe it is a mistake." I
was greatly relieved.

After I had finished my examination of its band, I held
the grackle in my hand some time longer. I admired the
iridescent purple of its neck and head; I was surprised
that such a cocky bird should be so subdued in captivity.
At last I let it go, and after the fact realized the opportun-
ity I had missed, the chance to draw it at close range.
Then and there I decided that future birds who tripped
our trap would pay for their indiscretion by sitting for
their portraits, at least the first of each kind. This led to
some interesting sessions, and the reactions of my subjects
varied widely. To show how different the subjects them-

selves were, here is the list of our captives as it appeared on the kitchen blackboard at the end of the 1969–70 trapping season:

Whitefooted Mouse	7	White-throated Sparrow	1
Gray Squirrel	7	Tree Sparrow	2
Red Squirrel	5	Fox Sparrow	1
Chipmunk	4	English Sparrow	1
Grackle	1	Chickadee	3
Bluejay	3	Tufted Titmouse	1
Junco	2		

The first bluejay was full of fight, and when I reached into the trap I used a glove. It was not a bit necessary, for the captive soon calmed down and was completely subdued. The next day I caught another and let it loose immediately. It streaked up into the trees on the back hill, from which safe retreat it screamed back imprecations. I guess there is a lot of bluff in the bluejay's bluster. It seems to prefer name-calling to fighting, and even that from a safe distance.

Most of the sparrows appeared uncomfortable but not overly perturbed. Before releasing one I showed my wife how to hypnotize a bird. I opened my hand so that it was lying on its back, feet in the air. She stroked its feathers, and for long minutes it lay there motionless. Then I turned it over slowly, and suddenly it came alive and dashed off. No bird has ever found itself on its back. It is a completely unnatural position, and so it simply lies there. This would not go on forever, of course. After a while it would begin to struggle and then discover that all was not as hopeless as it seemed.

The one exception to the general uneasiness of sparrows was the white-throat. Whether it was its natural reaction or whether it was because it was a young bird I shall never know, but it actually seemed to enjoy the whole thing. It did not struggle at all and was alert and interested in noises and movements while being held. When I was through and took it out on the back porch to let it go, it stood up on the palm of my hand and looked up at us as if to say, "Well, that was certainly an interesting experience." I actually had to toss it into the air before it would fly away. Add the name of white-throated sparrow to those of whitefooted mouse and flying squirrel as the most tractable and cooperative of wild creatures.

The real fighters were the chickadee and the titmouse, close cousins who evidently share the same temperaments. I should have worn a glove in handling the chickadee instead of the bluejay. It was mad all the way through, and took it out in a concentrated attack on my thumb. If you have watched a chickadee opening a sunflower seed, you can imagine how much power there is in those short, sharp stabs. It really hurt, and nothing but devotion to duty kept me from quitting halfway through the drawing.

The titmouse, on the other hand, was more indignant than mad. That was the first winter we had seen them with any regularity, a pair who always came in together and left together. We were very pleased that these southerners who were extending their range in the north had us on the list. When I saw there was a gray bird in the trap I thought it was a junco, but I brought it indoors anyway to take a look. When I opened the trap door the bird dashed past my reaching hand and flew headlong through the house, into the living room, the front hall, the dining room, until I finally caught it against the pantry window, an irate tufted titmouse. It did not act particularly frightened as I drew its picture. Its bill was closed and its crest semi-raised, and like the white-throat it was alert to noises and movements. However, it seemed to have an air of righteous indignation.

My journal for the following day, November 3, contains this query: "Today one titmouse showed up, only one. Until now they have always come in together. Wonder how long it will take the other to recover from the indignities it was subjected to yesterday?" The answer came sooner than I had expected. "November 6: We're forgiven! Or else titmice have a memory span of only four days. Today the pair came in together, and one hopped right into the trap, not once but twice. I feel sure it was the one who had not previously been humiliated. To forgive is not necessarily to forget."

It is December now, and so far we have had no occasion to set the trap under the feeder. However, cold weather has arrived and we have had our first snow. It is the time when any smart rodent comes indoors to a warm house. The last several nights there have been scurryings and gnawings in the partitions. I hope it is only whitefeet, but the pantry trap is set and so far has had no customers. So, on suspicion, the squirrel trap is ready and waiting at the top of the attic stairs. If we do have squirrels in the house, I hope it is as effective up there as it is out of doors.

SIX

Sounds in the Night

Some years ago, before children arrived to complicate our existence, we received the offer of a lifetime—the use of a friend's apartment in New York. She was off somewhere for a couple of weeks, and it was ours to use for the whole time or any part of it. We were elated. It was during the depression, and we could not possibly have afforded such a trip otherwise. We made a list of all the places we could see at little or no expense—museums, the Bronx Zoo, the Staten Island ferry, Fulton fish market—it went on and on. This was to be a vacation to remember.

We drove down, arriving about noon, and after locating the garage to which we had been directed, walked around

89

the corner to our home away from home. It could not
have been more centrally located, Madison Avenue near
Thirty-ninth Street, and it was on the second floor, a
beautiful studio apartment. We returned to it late that
evening after an exhausting start to our sightseeing tour,
all set for a good night's sleep. That was our mistake.

Traffic never lets up on Madison Avenue, and here it
was right under our windows, necessarily open in midsummer. Exhaust fumes poured into the room in noxious
waves, and at frequent intervals came the breathtaking
squeal of tires as two cars tried to avoid tangling with one
another. It was almost a relief to hear the sound of breaking glass and tearing metal. After all, you can hold your
breath just so long. There must have been a great deal of
crime in the streets, even in those days, for all night long
we heard the wail of sirens, police cars and fire apparatus
racing to a succession of emergencies. If they did not pass
directly under our windows it made little difference.
Their piercing shrieks were just as penetrating coming
from adjacent streets.

At long last came the dawn. Red-eyed and exhausted,
we stumbled about getting our breakfast, and at an early
hour doggedly resumed our tour. When we returned that
night, more tired than we ever remembered being before,
we were certain that nothing could possibly keep us
awake. Again we were wrong. It was a repeat of the night
before. The next morning we packed up and left for
home.

Some time later, maybe a year or so, we invited our New York friend to visit us. With memories of our short stay still fresh in our minds, we had a rather smug feeling as we thought of the relaxed, restful time she would have in the peace and quiet of the country. We were somewhat taken aback, therefore, to see her stumble downstairs for breakfast looking far from rested. However, we greeted her brightly with: "Well, did you have a good night's sleep?" Her answer left us without an adequate reply. "No, I couldn't sleep a wink, with those damn insects making such a racket!" Well, as the man says, it's all what you're used to.

The night sounds of summer are many and varied. Those that are identifiable are set against a background of insect orchestration, a melding of a thousand fiddlings and chirpings and raspings, which, to a sympathetic ear, is lulling music. Soloists frequently perform to this accompaniment—field crickets with their strident chirping, or snowy tree crickets spelling out the temperature by rubbing their wing files together. Hawthorne said that "if moonlight could be heard it would sound like that." Now and then a sleepy bird wakes long enough to break briefly into song. Or maybe it is singing in its sleep. I shall never know.

Animals of the night find good foraging in these outer suburbs. Where else is such a concentration of food provided by thoughtful householders as here? Certainly not in thinly settled rural areas. When we hear the sudden,

loud clang of our sunken garbage-pail cover, we know
that a raccoon is making its rounds. Sometimes a neighbor's dog comes across a coon, and then the night air is
filled with frenzied barks and savage snarls. Having seen
the size of some of these well-fed scavengers, they must
give most of our local dogs pause. They make formidable
antagonists.

Following the trail of the coons come the skunks. They
are not as choosy about their food, and there are always
leavings scattered around on the ground. Since skunks are
unable to open garbage-pail covers and since they have a
means of defense that does not necessitate fighting or
snarling, they add little to the sounds of the night. However, now and then I hear snuffling noises under my bedroom window, and I know the hunt is on for beetle grubs,
doing their evil worst to chew off all our grass roots.
Heaven knows our grass is being choked out fast enough
by invading weeds, without calling in beetle help to complete the job. Sure enough, the next morning the yard will
be pockmarked with shallow holes. Since each means one
less grub, we find no fault with their diggers. Skunks are
always welcome, as long as they confine their hunting to
the after-dark hours.

With the first frosts the insect chorus is stilled, although
not completely. A few hardy individuals survive, and on
warm nights that follow they try to repeat their earlier
performances. But it is a desultory attempt at best; a hand-
ful of players with out-of-tune instruments trying to emu-

late the sound of a full-fledged symphony orchestra. Soon they give it up, and the silent nights of late fall and winter are upon us. Maybe this is the time of year we should have invited our New York friend to visit us.

Winter nights are not completely silent, of course. In nature there is probably no such thing. Most sounds are muffled, like that made by fine snow filtering down through the cedar branches outside my window. Then there are the sharper more incisive sounds made by sleet. Jim Rowlands described it beautifully in *Cache Lake Country* as giving the impression of "tiny fingers picking at the panes." Occasionally, on a night of heavy snow or freezing rain, an overladen branch will give in with a sharp crack, and on sub-zero nights the cold may penetrate a limb and split it lengthwise with a report like a pistol shot.

Animal noises are rare in the deep of winter. Raccoons and skunks are asleep through the coldest weather. A January thaw may bring them out briefly, but when the mercury drops again, back they go. On occasion I have heard the sharp bark of a fox, maybe on a hunt, maybe challenging some comfort-loving dog to a game of chase through the deep snows of the back-hill woods. Once, and only once, I heard the death scream of a rabbit caught by a fox or an owl. I do not think I want to hear it again. It is the most blood-curdling scream I have ever heard, although I must admit to limited experience along this line. It sounds both human and inhuman at one and the same time, the

shrill, agonizing shriek of a lost soul bound to perdition.
No, I am sure I never want to hear it again.

The most frequently heard animal sounds of winter
nights, however, are the calls of owls. That is not to say
that they are heard so frequently as to be commonplace,
but I suspect we sleep through a great many performances. There are great horned owls in other parts of town,
but we have never heard them around our house. Barred
owls are not uncommon, and their hooting is unmistakable:
"hoohoo, hoohoo ... hoohoo, hoohoo-aw," two distinct
groups of four hoots each. Hence, one of its other names,
Eight-Hooter.

But by far the most common of the tribe is the little
screech owl, a misnomer if there ever was one. Records of
people who have actually heard this bird screech are
almost nonexistent. In fact, the only one I have come
across was when Forbush and Brewster, a couple of top-
flight field observers, heard a sound like "the first notes of
a siren whistle," and when it seemingly changed to the
familiar call of a screech owl, decided that was it. They
never saw the bird. In my journal there is this late fall
entry:

November 2: Sometime in the early morning hours, I
awoke to hear a soft, weird call coming from the woods
up back. At first it was too far away to identify surely,
then its maker came closer and the calling became
louder. It was a tremulous, quavering wail, the sort of
thing that should have been heard night before last, Hal-
lowe'en. It was a screech owl. Thoreau described its

eerie call as " . . . no honest and blunt tu-wit tu-who of the poets, but, without jesting, a most solemn graveyard ditty, the mutual consolations of suicide lovers remembering the pangs and the delights of supernal love in the infernal groves." I doubt that I would go quite that far, but it is certainly an other-worldly sound, especially in the hush of a black night. If hair can really be made to stand on end, this should do it.

To quote Thoreau still further, he puts words to that wailing: "Oh-o-o-o-o that I had never been bor-or-or-orn, comes faintly from far in the Lincoln woods." He would no doubt be pleased to know that, 130 years later, the Lincoln woods can still produce that sorry plaint. I have no idea who first misnamed this little owl, but it was at least as long ago as Pliny's time. He wrote: "The Scritch Owl always betokeneth some heavie news, and is most execrable and accursed." Possibly those Roman owls went in more for siren whistling. I wonder, though, if we should not give it a more appropriate name. There is one already in use down along the Gulf Coast. The Cajuns call it the "shivering owl."

The hushed nights of winter give way at last to the sometimes turbulent nights of spring. Instead of softly falling snow, pelting rains. Instead of tinkling sleet, gurgling rivulets coming down from the back hill, eating away at the snow cover which has stayed all too long. Instead of the crack of freezing branches, the thrilling clamor of high-flying geese heading north across a midnight sky.

And then the night arrives when we hear for the first time that long awaited sound, the call of the spring peepers. Weak and tentative at first, not quite sure that this is really the right time, if warm weather continues it soon becomes a full-throated chorus. They are in the wet places down at the foot of the hill some distance away, and it hardly seems possible that such a carrying call can be produced by tiny frogs, less than an inch long. But this thought rarely comes to mind as we hear the first peeper songs, joyous paeans of praise proclaiming that the frigid grip of winter has been broken and that spring is here at last.

Having reached this turning point of the seasons, we know that soon the night will be filled with the fiddlings and chirping and raspings of a thousand insects, the restful, lulling sounds of summer nights. Except, that is, for the ominous drone of an occasional mosquito who gets in around that left-hand window screen. It never has fitted quite right in thirty years. Some day I must get around to fixing it.

A Modest Flora

Since I am no botanist, I have never had the urge to refer to our plants and wildflowers by their scientific names: it would have added nothing to the beauty or the fragrance of their blossoms; I have had not reason for being too specific about their identification; and I do not consider a passing acquaintance with Latin nomenclature to be a sign of erudition. Furthermore, the books that I had readily available were either too sketchy or too encyclopedic to be of much help. The result has been a somewhat haphazard knowledge of our native flora.

99

I know well those wildflowers that are of special interst, the rare and secretive ones such as fringed gentians, cardinal flowers, trailing arbutus, and pitcher plants. We make pilgrimages each spring to search out bloodroots and the first hepaticas, unfolding their pale blue petals on sun-warmed slopes. But rank weeds and common flowers have done little to excite our curiosity. Any goldenrod was simply a goldenrod, any aster an aster. Then another addition to the Peterson guide series appeared, *A Field Guide to the Wildflowers*, and with it a changed point of view.

Like so many others, for years I have been in the habit of checking off every bird new to me on the life list in Peterson's *A Field Guide to the Birds*. There are similar lists in other books in this series, those on mammals, ferns, animal tracks, but there is none in the wildflower book. No doubt it would have taken up an unwarranted amount of space. But there is a perfectly good index which could serve the same purpose, so I began to check off those flowers which I was certain I had seen. Some went easily—adder's-tongue, trailing arbutus, arethusa, bee balm, and so on down to yucca. There were others, however, that gave pause. When you have always referred to every goldenrod by that one name, what do you do when confronted with a lineup of thirty different varieties? Or discover that, in addition to birdfoot violets, there are forty others? Obviously you make no check marks until you have taken some closer looks.

This kind of identification adds another dimension to flower appreciation. Our back hill takes on new interest in the fall when I realize that, hidden among those sere brown grasses, the inconspicuous blue-stemmed golden-rod is still in bloom. Even that pernicious weed of our so-called lawn which has always been known as "damn-hawkweed," now has a certain amount of interest since I discovered it is a variety known as mouse-ear hawkweed (often found in the company of mouse-ear chickweed). I find that name appealing, if not the plant. Then, too, there are nondescript weeds my earlier books would not deign to notice or at best pass off with a shrug, as I did also. Now I take a mild satisfaction in being able to say, with some assurance, "Oh, yes, the common speedwell."

The guide has also injected a game of sorts into our lives. On occasion my older daughter and I roam afield and try to stump one another on plants that are new to us. We are often successful. A few, in fact, we never find at all, more because of our ineptitude, no doubt, than from any fault in our bible. One that gave us some trouble for a while turned out to be a cypress spurge. Since this was a new family to us, we investigated further. Bailey's *Manual of Cultivated Plants* had this to offer: "Spurge Family, Euphorbiaceae. Herbs, shrubs, and trees of very diverse habits, some being fleshy and cactus-like; about 280 genera and over 8,000 species widely distributed around the world." Just how diverse this family is can be shown by naming just a few of its members: Chinese tung-oil tree; Para rubber tree; poinsettia; castor bean; snow-on-the-mountain; flowering spurge (dry soil, Ontario to Florida to Texas); and cypress spurge (culti-vated in old gardens and cemeteries). We found ours

beside a meandering path, so it was probably an escapee
from one of those old gardens, there being no cemeteries
nearby.

Peterson and his co-author, McKenny, cut that 8,000
figure down to size locally: "Species in our area, 57
(Gray), 55 (B&B)." Then they reduced those figures in
their own estimate to 37, of which only 7 are described in
the guide. We now have a satisfactory answer for any
plant whose identity eludes us, satisfactory to us, at least.
"Why it's a spurge, obviously." Considering their numbers
and diversity, we could even be right.

There is little, if anything, to excite the interest of a
horticulturist in the flora of our yard. There is variety, yes,
but mostly the variety of common things—black-eyed
Susans, cowpeas (or, more properly, cow vetch), violets,
and forsythia in such quantity that we can never keep
them pruned back. There are a few plants that have special significance for us. The short line of pennyroyal at the
edge of the patio brings back boyhood memories of the
family farm in Maine. At the foot of one hayfield, along
the edge of my favorite trout brook, was a considerable
stand of this redolent mint. Rubbing a few leaves between
my fingers today provides immediate transport to those
long-gone days when bare feet did the crushing and that
delicious, all-pervasive odor filled the still summer air.
Then all the world was young and full of wonder and
promise. To recapture something of that feeling, even for
a fleeting moment, is a rare and treasured experience.

There is an iris growing in the corner of what once was
our upper garden. Each spring it pushes up through a

tangle of grass and weed roots and produces one flower
stalk. The deep purple blossoms are beautiful but hardly a
rarity. Yet this lone plant has special meaning for us.
When our youngest was four or five she decided it was
high time she had her own garden. She made no little
plans, but had in mind a mixed flower and vegetable
garden of some size and variety. "And you won't have to
worry, Daddy. I'll take care of it all myself." It took a considerable amount of diplomacy, but at last she settled for
one corner of the garden in which to plant an iris and a
few unremembered companions requiring almost no care.
Today, almost twenty years later, our garden has returned
to its native state, and with it went hers, except for that
iris. We look foward each year to greeting again those
blossoms about which we were not to worry, reminders
that in a world of change some things do remain constant.

We remember clearly the tangle of rank weeds that formerly grew in the shade of the lilacs, barberries, and forsythia marking our northern property line. Now they are
gone, and the ground is covered with a thick layer of bark
mulch and pine needles. In early spring violets push up
through it, Canada, lance-leaved, and northern downy.
There are a few hepaticas, wintergreen, and spreading
patches of partridgeberries. We hope the shinleaf, tril-
liums, and arbutus we put in last year will survive. And
after the early flowers come the ferns, thriving in the
shade and keeping down the unwanted weeds. They are
common ferns, Christmas, woodsia, cinnamon, and royal,
but they are green and beautiful and very satisfactory.

We also remember denuded slopes where nothing grew

and which are now covered with thick mats of myrtle and
ivy and occasional islands of false Solomon's seal, English
apple mint, and ferns. In one instance, beside the patio,
such a once-barren slope now boasts a lush growth of
day lilies, whose blossoms range in color from light yellow
to dark red, almost black, and whose blooming season
extends from early spring to midsummer. Our "exotica"
we call them, and they deserve the name. To see a tiger
swallowtail dipping into the nectaries of a deep red lily is
a sight long remembered.

Our flowers, both wild and cultivated, interest us
because of familiarity and associations. I think on occasion how much apartment dwellers miss, those people
who, in the words of Edwin Way Teale, "move from shell

to shell like hermit crabs." They are people who have no roots, for whom there is no pennyroyal, no purple iris, no exotica. I know very well that an affluent hermit crab living in his luxurious pearl-lined shell will resent a proffer of sympathy from anyone. Nonetheless, I offer it gratuitously.

Although our weeds and wildflowers are lacking in both variety and numbers, the same cannot be said of our tree flowers. I rather suspect that most people, if asked to name the flowering trees of their acquaintance, would begin with "apple, horse chestnut, flowering dogwood . . ." and would soon exhaust their acquaintanceships. Yet they could have gone on and on, for all our trees are flowering trees. The great majority, however, bear flowers so inconspicuous that they go unnoticed by most. The Norway maple that spreads all the way across our lower lawn has countless thousands of blooms each spring. But they are small, visible only at close range, and since they are the same yellow-green as the young leaves that appear along with them, they are effectively hidden. The tiny flowers of an elm look like floral arrangements in little baskets, but seen from the ground they only give the twigs a fuzzy appearance, softening the stark outlines of winter. White ash has yellow pompoms, birches drooping catkins, pines clusters of fat spikes filled with pollen. All are different, but with one thing in common. Except for the few flamboyant ones, most tree blossoms go unnoticed and unknown.

If few people know tree blossoms, fewer still realize

how well developed their buds are long before they are called upon to open by the warm urgings of spring. Anyone who stops to consider must surely realize that buds do not suddenly come into being at the end of winter and burst into bloom or leaf overnight. If there are such misconceptions, it is simply because few people have ever given it any thought. The fact of the matter is that buds spend the growing months of each year developing, remain dormant during the cold months of winter, and burst their bonds the following spring. Some produce flowers, some leaves, many both, and they are well developed by late summer, perfect miniatures, neatly wrapped and encased in tough protective coatings. I cut some open in November, buds of lilac, horse chestnut, and flowering dogwood. Under a microscope the end bud of the lilac showed round flower buds packed tight around their central stem. The horse chestnut bud showed the same compact arrangement of flowers, protected by woolly packing and wrapped in leaves. Flowers and leaves would emerge together. The fat shoebutton bud of the flowering dogwood is unique. Its outer shell is in four sections. When they open in the spring and the inconspicuous flower clusters are exposed to view, instead of falling off as do most protective caps, those segments are pushed out on the ends of creamy white or pink bracts, the showy "petals" surrounding the flowers. The original segments remain, unchanged in size or color. They are the little dark blotches at the notched ends of the bracts.

The plants and flowers of our yard may be an undistinguished lot, but that is not to say they are lacking in interest, especially to us who know them well. Each spring we look for the half-dozen or so miniature tulips that have come up for years in one corner of the garden. We regularly wonder what that little plant with the spotted leaves and pink-blue flowers can be that comes up behind the garage. Someone gave it to us years ago, but now both the name of the giver and the gift have been forgotten. Some day we may succeed in identifying it, but in the meantime there is a certain amount of pleasure in having a mystery plant. We know that those big pink milkweed blossoms on the back hill, so beautiful to us, are deadly traps to numbers of small insects. And we know, too, that if we lift our eyes above the ground at the right time of year, a whole new flowering world will be opened up to us. Yes, ours is a modest flora. It will never be included in anyone's wildflower garden tour, but we would not have it any other way. To us, and to our wild neighbors with whom we share it, it is eminently satisfying.

EIGHT

The Transients

November 29. The fox sparrows must have moved on. We have had a half dozen of them for the last two weeks, stopping over on their way south. As long as the weather stayed reasonably mild and the food plentiful, they were in no great hurry to leave. Although this morning is almost balmy, that 20 degree spell we had yesterday was probably the nudge they needed to move on.

We always look forward to seeing fox sparrows. Twice the size of tree sparrows, with big chestnut splotches on their breasts, they are striking birds. Each spring and fall they visit us on their way through, like old friends who drop in briefly to enjoy our hospitality. For a few days

109

they are here, scratching through the grass for fallen seeds, then they are gone. We know, however, they will return in a few months, and when they do winter will be over. They are welcome transients at any season, but especially so in the spring.

Invariably the fox sparrows are accompanied by white-throated sparrows. Not that they travel together, necessarily, but they arrive and depart at about the same time. Both of these birds breed as far north as Labrador, and spend their winters all the way from southern New England to the Gulf of Mexico, and they take their time about making the trip. Some birds seem to feel that once they have started their migration they have to get it over with in a hurry. These two sparrows look much fatter and happier for taking it in easy stages.

On a day in May we were out in the apple orchard beside the house. This was when it was truly an apple orchard, before it was allowed to fall into neglect and be taken over by hordes of maples. It was apple-blossom time, and although they were to be followed by completely inedible fruit, the blossoms were superb. As we stood there admiring the clouds of pink and white against a clear blue sky, a long-winged bird swooped across our vision. It flew low over the trees and disappeared before we really got a good look at it. While we were still wondering what we had seen, another came into view, then another and another. The sky seemed full of them, swooping, wheeling, turning, climbing, and when we saw the white patches like windows on their wings, we knew they were nighthawks, on their way back from a South American winter. We had no idea how many there were in the flight. In the middle of the orchard our vision was restricted. There might have been a dozen, or just as readily a hundred. It was pure guesswork. The chimney swifts, also South American vacationers, had preceded them by a week or so. These two are among nature's most efficient exterminators of flying insects. We could wish that the nighthawks, like the swifts, would stay with us. A few do, but most have discovered that we have nothing to offer comparable to the great clouds of mosquitoes in the northern tundra. Many get as far north as the Yukon, aerial transients over our back yard en route.

The fox sparrows and white-throats stay with us long enough so they can hardly be missed. However, had we not been outdoors at just the right time, we would never have known that the nighthawks had gone through. Undoubtedly we miss a great many more casual visitors, those who arrive in small numbers and are gone before they are noticed or secretive birds who manage to stay well hidden.

One day in late October I had a good example of the sort of fortuitous timing that is all too rare. I had stepped out on the back porch for a moment when I heard thin, lisping sounds up on the back hill. In the leafless upper branches of the ash, a dozen or so birds talked quietly as they fluttered from one perch to another. I had to get the glasses to discover that they were cedar waxwings, not their usual sleek selves but all fluffed out against the cold

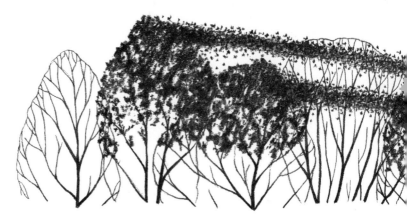

of a raw, drizzly day. They knew they had overstayed their leave, and were headed for warmer climes. When I looked again, a few minutes later, they had gone.

Time and again we have heard the chirpings and twitterings of many small birds in the maple orchard or in the evergreens on the back hill. We might see movement now and then as they flitted back and forth through the thick growth, but never get a clear look at one. It is very frustrating. And then there are birds who cannot possibly be overlooked, who demand to be noticed.

It was a gray, rainy morning in late March, and I was up and about well before dawn, as is my custom. Shortly after sunrise I was aware of a great clamoring outside. I looked out the pantry window to discover that the tops of the maples on the back hill were alive with grackles, hundreds and hundreds of them. The bare limbs had suddenly come alive with a clacking, creaking multitude. For some reason they had congregated in only three trees. It seemed as though no one of them could possibly hold any more birds, but then another flight of a hundred or so

would sweep over our roof and settle in among the others. Flight after flight did the same thing. Evidently overcrowding was something to be desired. The new contingents were swallowed up in the black mass. It was so dense in the beginning that a few hundred more made no noticeable change. For five or ten minutes this went on, and the noise was deafening. Then a few took off toward the west, then a few more, and then an increasing stream until suddenly the trees were bare again. The black cloud had disappeared and the silence was almost oppressive. While getting accustomed to it I could not help feeling sorry for a lot of people on the other side of town who were being rudely awakened from a sound sleep. No, the black-grackle hordes cannot possibly be overlooked.

Early one Easter morning I glanced out the dining room window as I consulted the indoor-outdoor thermometer, and noticed a foreign object under the cedar at the corner of the house. It was still too dark under those low-hanging branches to see what it was. It could have been a stone or a clod of earth, but whatever it was it had not been there the day before. Then it moved and I saw that it was a bird, a chunky bird with a long bill and short legs, and then I knew that the woodcock flight was on. Unlike the noisy grackles, woodcock are secretive birds. They migrate at night, spending their days foraging for food. Since their wings are short, they probably expend a good deal of energy in distance flights. Under normal living conditions a woodcock eats at least its own weight in earthworms every day, so how much more food must it need during migration. They seem to drop off, exhausted, wherever a bit of green holds promise of providing food. A friend living on Charles Street in the middle of Boston was surprised one morning to discover a woodcock in his postage-stamp back yard.

this one did nothing but sleep. He might have been called a sedentary grouse. I suppose there are plenty of ruffed grouse in the woods behind the house. The hill is covered with a thick growth including some really big pines and hemlocks, with partridgeberries and other attractive forage on the forest floor. But the grouse that must surely live there have never ventured down into our yard before, at least as far as we knew. At first glance this bird had no more form than the woodcock had when I first spotted it, but I knew very well no stone or clod of earth would be perched halfway up the cedar in the side yard. Besides, it looked more like a balloon topped with a small crest.

It would be a gross exaggeration to say that our visit from the ruffed grouse afforded us much entertainment. For the better part of the day he sat there, and for some time I sat at the bedroom window with my sketch pad at the ready, waiting to record his every move. The balloon pose was one; same with neck extended was two; and a perfunctory bit of preening was three. That exhausted his repertoire. It was pleasant to have had him as a temporary guest, but as I say, he did little to liven our day.

Not all of our occasional visitors are happy about being here. Some of those who show up in late fall or early winter would much prefer to be far to the south. These are the birds who were left behind in migration. They were sick or injured at the time, and when they recuperated all their friends had gone and they, themselves, had lost the migratory urge. Many, especially the insect eaters, do not last long. But there are other and hardier birds who make the best of a bad situation. There are always

overwintering robins who live in sheltered areas such as cedar swamps and subsist on berries. One that showed up in midwinter had three or four broken primary feathers sticking out from his wing, his reason for missing migration. Yet he looked fat and perky, and flew off with no apparent difficulty. I was a bit concerned about a December hermit thrush, but then I remembered its close relationship to the robins and decided it would probably come through all right.

There seemed to be no ray of hope, however, for the brown thrasher that appeared after an early January thaw. The winter had been fairly open up to that point, and the thaw exposed green patches here and there. The thrasher poked through them in a desultory manner, then flew up on the patio roof and ate a few bittersweet berries. It seemed listless and forlorn. That night there was a freezing rain, and the next day everything was encased in a hard coating of ice. I doubt if the thrasher survived that storm. At least we never saw it again.

These words are being written in late October. The first killing frost came a week ago. The dead tomato plants were stripped from the feeder post that had been their mainstay all summer, the feeder reinstalled on top, and mixed seed spread on the ground beneath. The seed was left over from last season, and over summer had picked up an active insect population, providing our birds with a more or less balanced diet. Today, for the first time, two fox sparrows appeared. We know that the white-throats will not be far behind. This chapter has come full circle.

The Peaceful Garden

It was a hot midday in midsummer. The topmost leaves of
the maples moved slightly in upper breezes that rarely
reached down into the garden. Even the tallest flowers
were motionless on their long stalks. If it was a bit too hot
and humid for humans, it was ideal for insects. The air
was alive with them. Butterflies of all sorts and sizes, from
beautiful swallowtails to sulphurs and skippers, flitted
from blossom to blossom. They were joined by countless
smaller insects, bees, wasps, and flies, each busy with its

119

own affairs. It was a calm, peaceful scene, an oasis of tranquillity in a world of turmoil and strife. But it was a deceptive peace. In this quiet garden lurked strange killers and sudden death.

A brown skipper flitted restlessly from one dwarf marigold to another. Maybe the nectaries of these blossoms had already been depleted by the hordes of busy insects, although this was highly improbable. Butterflies are apt to be choosy, and not as serious about their work as some. Bees tend strictly to business and put in a full day's work. Butterflies, on the other hand, spend a large part of their time moving aimlessly from place to place, swirling up in the air with a companion in play, or simply resting on a broad leaf or warm fence rail, opening and closing their wings as though demanding to be admired.

The skipper was no great beauty, in fact it was rather drab and colorless, but it had inherited the restlessness of its kind. It flew across to the cutting garden, to the inviting heads of big zinnias, calendulas, and giant marigolds. It paid a brief visit to a zinnia, now past its prime, then skipped across to a marigold, a beckoning ball of brilliant yellow-orange. Alertly it stepped across the ruffled petal-like bracts to the tightly bunched florets in their center and thrust its long, hollow tongue down the tubes of one after another in quick succession.

As the little butterfly worked its way across the packed flower heads it failed to see what lay in wait on the far side. For days a crab spider had frequented this particular marigold. It had found a good spot and there was no

reason to go elsewhere. Squatting motionless at the edge of the massed flowers, its yellow color not far different from that of the frilly blossom, it was almost invisible. Its front legs, two on each side, were grotesquely long. When the skipper landed they had been stretched out to the spider's sides, but immediately they were pulled up over its back, ready and waiting to strike. It was like setting a steel trap. A battery of eight eyes watched the unsuspecting prey draw closer and closer, and then, suddenly, the trap was sprung. Sharp, pointed claws snapped shut on the furry body and held it in an unbreakable grip. Too late the skipper tried to escape, its wings beating wildly. The spider's front claws held its victim tight, while the four short legs kept a firm grip on the blossom.

The struggle was short. Sharp fangs pierced the butterfly's body, and numbing poison was pumped into it. The wings beat more and more feebly, and when they were finally stilled the killer settled down to enjoy its meal. Now, as the skipper's body juices were sucked in, the spider began to swell. Before its victim had been discarded, an empty shell, the trapper looked like a yellow balloon.

In a nearby blossom another trapper waited patiently. It was a tiny insect, no more than a third of an inch long. Its irregular shape had no distinct outline, and its yellow and black coloring matched the light and shade of the marigold head. Lying in wait at the edge of the nectar-laden florets, the ambush bug blended into its surroundings in an almost perfect example of camouflage.

In spite of its diminutive size, seen through the eyes of

another small insect the ambush bug has a frightening, almost nightmarish appearance. From its clublike antennae and bulging eyes back to its winged body, the entire forward part of the insect is armor plated, impervious to the stings and bites of struggling captives. Its front legs are broad and thick, with needle-tipped claws that clamp against the serrated edges of the legs with a viselike grip. Anchored firmly by its other four feet, the little ambush bug is capable of subduing bees and butterflies many times its size, and its strong sucking beak soon stills their struggles.

There is a third insect which makes the flower heads its hunting grounds, but this one does not lie in wait. Not much larger than the ambush bugs, assassin bugs stride slowly across the massed bracts and petals, ready to seize any small insect they might come across. Adult assassin bugs have wings and long, jointed sucking beaks. The young, or nymphs, are wingless, but their beaks are just as sharp and just as effective. It stretches the imagination to compare our garden with an African veldt, but the assassin bugs stalk their prey in just the same way as do lions. Raising one foot after another, so slowly it hardly seems to move at all, the hunter advances. At last, when it has reached striking distance, the front legs suddenly lash out to grasp the hapless victim and the sharp beak pierces its body. There is one disadvantage, of course, in this slow-motion approach. A restless insect may, and often does, take off before the hunter has completed its stalk. But if it cannot win them all, the successes seem to occur

often enough to keep it well fed. At least I have yet to see
an assassin bug that appeared to be particularly ema-
ciated.

It must not be supposed that these insects confine their
activities to our garden. Every wildflower bouquet we
bring in from the back hill, whether goldenrod or black-
eyed Susans or Queen Anne's lace, or probably a happy
combination, is certain to have its quota of insects who
soon start to wander about the house. When I look up
from my chair at the flowers hanging over me from their
place on the bookcase, I am not in the least surprised to
see an assassin bug advancing over the top of the chair
wing, a harmless looking little green insect. I get it to step
onto my hand, then take it to the back porch and let it
loose, to get on with the business of hunting down other
insects, noxious ones, I hope.

There seem to be almost as many ways of catching prey
as there are insects. While the crab spiders wait in
ambush, the orb-weavers spin webs to trap their food
supply. The big black and yellow garden spiders wait in
the middle of their webs for flying or leaping insects to
become entangled. There are other spiders, some beautifully marked, who spin their webs, then retreat to the
concealment of an overhanging leaf. Here they lie in wait,
each holding a line fastened to its web's center, like a fisherman waiting for a bite. When an insect is entrapped the
line vibrates, and the fisherman quickly descends to wrap
its catch in a silken shroud. Then, cut loose from the web,
it is carried back to the hiding place to be dehydrated at

leisure. Down in the grass are numbers of small webs whose makers wait at the bottom of centrally placed tunnels. During the day these webs are almost impossible to see, but in early morning after a damp night they stand out in all their dewcovered beauty, the "fairy tablecloths" which so delight small children.

We have never had any black widows in our yard, which is probably just as well. When the children were young it would certainly have been a strain on our peace of mind. They are not unknown in the neighborhood, although they are far from common. A friend called one day to ask me to identify a suspect. Sure enough, in a tangled mass of thread under the overhang of a big boulder behind her house, was a black-widow spider and her egg sac. I collected both and brought them home, where the spider was thoroughly photographed from all angles. If she was typical, I find it difficult to imagine how anyone could possibly be bitten by one. When I nudged her with a pencil to get her to move into a better position, she invariably folded her legs and collapsed. Rarely have I seen a more timid creature.

In due course the eggs hatched, and hundreds of tiny black spiders scurried about the inside of the jar. For several days I watched their numbers dwindle as the little cannibals ate one another, and finally I donated the mother and her remaining young to the Museum of Science. I understand they were quite a hit for the rest of the season, traveling around to summer camps along with an assortment of snakes, a porcupine, a great horned owl, and other unfamiliar and awesome creatures. I never did find out how many, if any, of the young survived the attentions of their bloodthirsty siblings.

Then there are the hunting spiders. Although we seldom see wolf spiders, I feel sure it is only because they see us first. They prefer wooded areas to mowed lawns, but we have enough trees of all sorts surrounding us to qualify. Some of these hunters build tunnels in the ground, sallying forth at night to do their foraging. If there are such tunnels in our yard I have yet to find them. Our wolf spiders hunt in the open, running down their quarry like the fierce beasts for which they are named.

Having no established base, the females are forced to carry their egg sacs around with them, suspended beneath their bodies. If it seems a bit awkward to carry on a chase with this impediment, how much more so must it be when the eggs hatch, for then the young clamber up onto their mother's back. It is a formidable sight to see a wolf spider with its body seemingly swollen to several times its normal size. She carries the spiderlings about in this fashion for a considerable time, but if they slow her down appreciably it makes little difference. There are always caterpillars and other insects which are incapable of making speedy escapes.

We also have a number of varieties of jumping spiders, none of which grow to any great size. They are alert little creatures, constantly swiveling about on the lookout for a prospective meal. They have short, hairy legs, and some are very colorful. Most spiders have eight eyes, simple eyes or ocelli arranged in different ways. Crab spiders and web builders have no use for distance seeing, and their eyes are small with limited vision. Wolf and jumping spiders, however, must of necessity see well. One pair of eyes, looking forward, are larger than the others, much larger in the case of jumping spiders. They look for all the world like great headlights.

There is nothing hit or miss about a jumping spider's hunting. It does not leap wildly into space after a prospective victim. Rather, it approaches slowly until within easy reach, then jumps quickly and surely. Nor does it take any chances of falling through space. Just before jumping it fastens an anchor line of silk to its take-off spot. If it fails to find a foothold at the end of the leap, it swings safely on this line, then climbs back up to its former perch.

Although it does not frequent the garden, there is one trapper who cannot be overlooked. Our stair landing between the first and second floors necessitated building a

projection on the side of the house, and the ground underneath it is protected from all but the most driving rains.
As a consequence the dirt in this small area is dry and
powdery, an ideal situation for the ant lions whose funnel
traps pockmark its surface. They lie in wait at the bottom
of their conical pits, toothed pincerlike jaws ready to
clamp onto ants or other hapless insects who tumble
down the steep sides. When the children were small no
year went by without an ant-lion colony in a glass tank
decorating the kitchen table for at least part of the
summer.

There are many interesting things about ant lions, some
of them unique. Consider the name, for a starter. To the
best of my knowledge it is the only insect whose adult
form is named after the larva. The long-bodied
gossamer-winged insect is known simply as an adult ant
lion. Then there is the peculiarity of its digestive system.
Ant lions do not defecate, and their rate of growth is
entirely a function of the availability of food. If it is plentiful, they grow fast and soon pupate. If it is scarce, they
simply wait it out as long as is necessary, with no shrink-
age of their bodies between meals. It is rather like filling a
jug of water. It makes no difference whether it is done
speedily or slowly, as long as it gets filled.

Digging the trap is a fascinating process. When a thick
layer of dry, sandy dirt had been laid in the glass-sided
case, we uprooted two or three ant lions and introduced
them to their new home. They have soft, flat bodies,
shaped something like pumpkin seeds, rather small heads,

and needle-sharp curved mandibles like a pair of calipers. They evidently have a great dislike of being out in the open, for immediately they went to work digging pits. Moving backward, their rear ends digging into the dirt like scoops, they went around and around in circles. As the dirt filtered down onto their heads, a quick flip sent it flying off to the side. Succeeding circles were smaller than the previous ones, and in a surprisingly short time each digger had made a perfect conical pit, the sides at just the right slope to keep the dirt from sliding down. Then the insects backed into the bottom of their pits until only those deadly mandibles were showing.

I must admit we always had something of a guilt complex when we sent ant after ant to its doom. But we managed to override it, and the ant lions were well fed. When an ant stumbled over the edge of a pit and started to slide down, it immediately tried to scramble back to the top. The angle was so steep it probably would not have made it anyhow, but the trapper was taking no chances. It sent up shower after shower of dirt to help speed the descent, and in short order those fierce jaws had clamped tight on its victim. The meal took little time as the juices flowed from ant to ant lion, and soon the dried husk was flipped up out of the pit, and the trap was set all over again.

I have always regretted that we do not have one of the most interesting and appealing of all insects, the praying mantis, in our yard. We are a bit north of their usual range, but they have been found in town on occasion, and I have seen them up into New Hampshire. We have cer-

tainly tried. I have turned full-grown mantes loose, and
they have just disappeared. One year I got an egg mass,
kept it until the young hatched, then released them in the
garden. There must have been well over a hundred, and
for several days I searched the area where I had let them
go, finding fewer and fewer each time. At last there were
none, and I never saw any of them again.

Once, at a garden party, we witnessed an unusual occur-
rence. One of the guests who was wearing a dress with
large green leaves on a white background, came up to me
saying, "Look what I found." Sitting on one of the big
leaves was a praying mantis, looking very much at home.
Maybe that is what we should do. If I could only induce
my wife to spend more time sitting out on the patio in a
dress decorated with large green leaves, it might do the
trick. At least we have tried everything else. Or maybe we
should just settle for the hunters and trappers we now
have. Possibly watching them does something to satisfy
that age-old hunting instinct which normally lies dormant
in most of us.

TEN

Oddly Enough

Most of our birds and beasts and insectivorae behave in what is, for them, a perfectly normal manner. The chickadees spend most of their time visiting our feeders or hunting through the trees for insects. The red squirrels are usually on the go, up and down the pine or along their well-traveled paths through the treetops. And the insects are all doing what comes naturally to them, hunting other insects, pollinating flowers, building nests, rearing young, singing, all the multitudinous pursuits of their kind. But every now and then our wild neighbors step out of character and do the unusual. Or, if it is not unusual to them, it seems so to us. The sight of a fighting-mad cottontail, a cigar-smoking red squirrel, or a pheasant crowing from a precarious perch high in the pine tree, these certainly appear to be unique performances.

Consider that pugilistic rabbit for a starter. It was a day in June, a perfectly normal day otherwise. We were starting out the front door when we were stopped by the curious behavior of a bluejay on the lower lawn. It would leap into the air, land a short distance away, and almost immediately fly up again. We soon saw the why of this acrobatic exercise, but we found it hard to believe. It was being harassed by a fighting rabbit, obviously bent on mayhem. This was completely absurd. A cottontail is one of the most timid creatures in the world. Its only defense lies in keeping out of sight or running away. The mad March Hare of the famed Tea Party was mentally deranged, but here before our eyes was a physically mad rabbit.

The chase continued for several minutes. Then the jay, either admitting defeat or tiring of the whole thing, flew off, and the cottontail was lost from sight under the upper slope. We went to the top of the slope and looked down, but there was no sign of the victorious battler.

Several days went by before I discovered the reason for that unlikely display. Among the mixed growth on the upper slope is a healthy stand of English apple mint, and it was ready for the season's first cutting, with mint jelly in mind. As I worked my way along the slope I came across a half-hidden hole, hardly more than a depression. Parting the myrtle I saw that it was lined with soft rabbit

hair, and on the lawn just below was where we had witnessed the jay-rabbit confrontation. Either the jay had
discovered this hidden retreat with its clutch of helpless
young cottontails, or the watchful mother was afraid it
would. In any event the result was the same, and the
intruding menace was driven off. This may be perfectly
normal procedure for a cottontail under the circum-
stances, but to us it was a once-in-a-lifetime sight, abnor-
mal enough to be included in our catalogue of oddities.

There is nothing new or novel about robins chasing
bluejays, especially during the nesting season. It happens
all the time. I did, however, witness one such chase that
ended in a most peculiar manner. One late May afternoon
I was working at the kitchen table when I became con-
scious of a great flashing of wings outside the window. I
looked up in time to see a bluejay do a bit of aerobatics
rather like a half loop, then land under the feed tray and
begin to gather up seeds. I assumed it had been a pair of
jays engaged in fun and frolic, and half rose from my
chair to see if the other was there, too. Then I discovered
it was no jay but a cock robin, and in a most unusual pose.
He was maybe ten feet from the jay, standing with his
back turned and his tail feathers spread wide, and he was
maintaining a fixed stare over his shoulder. Then he did
something I have never seen any bird other than an owl
or long-necked ducks and geese do, he turned his head so
that it pointed directly down the middle of his back. For
some minutes he held that pose and then, possibly con-
vinced he had accomplished his purpose, flew away, probably to resume his post as guardian of the nest. I feel sure

a behavioral biologist would have a ready name and explanation for this performance, something like the "Reverse Threat Posture coupled with the Spread-Fan Display. Both are first and foremost hostile, and are indicative of both attack and escape tendencies." I am certainly not going to argue with a behavioral biologist, even an imaginary one.

May 11: A COCK CROWS AT DAWN

It seems to me there is something quite wrong about a cock crowing and a crow cawing. Why should a crow be denied the privilege of calling out its own name? "Crow, crow, crow—here I am." Chickadees do it, so do phoebes and chewinks. It seems like a form of discrimination, although I would be the last to make an issue of it. There is far too much of that sort of thing already. However, all that aside, our dawns are usually greeted by either cawings or crowings. This morning it was both.

Crows often stop off in our pine tree on their way to parts unknown. One did so this morning in the gray of early dawn. Invariably a crow announces its presence with a few harsh calls, but this one went on and on, as though something was disturbing it. An owl, perhaps, or a hawk? I went to the window and looked up. It was neither. Perched high in the upper branches was a cock pheasant. It was some time before sunrise, but the lightening eastern sky made his chestnut vest shine out against the dark sky behind him. Then, as I watched in amazement, he stood up straight on the slim branch, flapped his wings, and crowed lustily. The effort was almost too much on that precarious perch, but with some quick footwork and seesaw balancing, he succeeded in staying upright. I can't think this peculiar treetop display really unsettled the crow, but at any rate, it left immediately for other and saner parts.

On rare occasions I have seen pheasants in trees, always before in winter when they were feasting on frozen fruits. Probably some spend their nights or sit out storms roosting in thick evergreens, but pheasants are ground birds. They have very short hind toes, not at all adapted for clasping branches. This bird, however, seemed to be up there for no other reason than that he enjoyed it. I watched him for about twenty minutes, during which time he crowed often, and always with the same loss of balance. He seemed perfectly happy, whether standing or sitting, either across the branch or lengthwise, and he was constantly changing position. With all the big limbs available, I could not help wondering why he had chosen such a small branch. It was no more than an inch thick. Maybe he considered it a challenge. Or maybe he wanted altitude to prove to his mate, down below somewhere brooding her eggs, that he was truly lord of all he surveyed. "Some cocks crow from compost heaps, but look—look at me!"

We have no pear tree and this was no partridge, but we are perfectly willing to settle for a pheasant in a pine tree as another of our rarities.

Possibly the vision of the cigar-smoking squirrel should come under some such heading as optical illusions. I must say it was a rather startling sight. A red squirrel had paused in its travels along a pine branch and was sitting up to take a momentary respite. It was silhouetted against the late afternoon sky and there was no question about it, the squirrel was smoking a big, black cigar. A picture of contentment, its front paws were folded across its chest, its plume of a tail rose over its back, and an outsized stogie was clamped firmly in its mouth. All that was needed to make the picture complete was a puff of smoke.

This year we have had a bumper crop of pine cones. When our tree shed its last needles of the year, the cones came down too. The ground was littered with them, long and thin, their pitchy scales clamped tight. The squirrels know full well that there are tasty seeds hidden under those scales, and they are laying in a supply for winter. I had paid no attention to the way in which they were being carried, however, until I saw that startling apparition against the sky.

These cones are anywhere from three to six inches long,

and some are an inch thick in the middle. A squirrel's mouth can stretch just so far, and it is only logical that it should seize the smallest part of the cone, the end. We have now become accustomed to seeing cigar-carrying squirrels, but I shall always remember my astonishment at seeing that first contented smoker. In this day and age when cigar makers are trying all sorts of tricks to win converts, including flavoring their product to taste like anything but tobacco—menthol, wild cherry, even blueberry—have they overlooked something? Maybe a pine-flavored cigar would be an overnight sensation. The squirrels, at least, would think so.

Elsewhere I have written of the breakneck speed with which our red squirrels flash up and down the pine, especially when they are engaged in the amatory pursuits of spring. Even more amazing are those times when they travel upside down on the bottom of limbs. It does not happen often, and probably only from necessity, not choice. When a limb is covered with a thick cap of snow which, in turn, is encased in ice, there is no other route possible. I reason that they always have a firm grip with at least two feet, like a fly walking on a ceiling. But how can one explain a bird in the same situation?

One winter day I watched a downy woodpecker hitch his way along the underside of a limb, every bit as casually as if he were climbing a tree trunk. He would let go with both feet and advance an inch or more each time. There was no fluttering assistance from his wings, and his progress seemed effortless and assured. What had hap-

pened to the force of gravity? Why, in that brief moment
when he had no contact whatsoever with the bark, did he
not fall? I kept telling myself that as he hitched forward
he also pushed up, but there was certainly no evidence of
it. He seemed to be hopping along just as naturally as he
would had he been right-side up, just as though there
were unseen gyros like a fly's halteres to keep him on an
even keel.

I feel sure there are ornithologists with a ready answer
to my problem. Maybe I shall ask one sometime—on
second thought, maybe not. I find it rather pleasant to
have unanswered mysteries of no real moment like this.
There would be little wonder left in life if we knew—or
thought we knew—all the answers.

There was certainly no mystery about the chickadees'
shower bath. They were simply having fun. Toward the
end of a hot summer's day, I went out to save our garden
from complete dehydration by giving it a thorough
drenching. This is not a task I find particularly onerous in
such weather. The hose nozzle leaks profusely, and when
held strategically over bare feet, both the garden and the
gardener benefit from its cooling effect. On this particular
afternoon there were other beneficiaries.

At first there was only one chickadee. It flew down onto
a day lily stalk to see what was going on. I was using a
fine spray and I raised the stream slightly to give my visitor a light shower. It flew up into the willows, but a
moment later came back again. Then others came flocking
in to join it. At first they simply watched, but then they

got into the spirit of the thing, swooping down through the spray and up into the cedar, then back through again and up into the lilacs. Some of the more acrobatically inclined did loops in midstream, doubling back to their starting points. They lit on the edge of the bird bath and let the drops shower down on them, and all the while they kept up a constant chattering. It was undoubtedly the same family that had been around the backyard for a week or more. There were probably no more than a half dozen or so, but in the confusion of all that flitting back and forth it seemed like many more.

I have always thought that chickadees have more fun than anybody, and now I am sure of it. But what I fail to understand is why they never did it again. They obviously had such a good time I was sure it would become a regular habit. Yet although the hose and I were there day after day and the chickadees were around at all hours, they never returned for another shower bath. Why? Having found a good thing, it would seem only logical that they would become regular bathers. So maybe there is a mystery of sorts here after all.

If our wild friends never stepped out of character, if all their movements and actions were predictable, they would make dull watching. Fortunately this is not so. You never know when a rabbit will become a lion, or a ground bird will reach for the heights. These odd moments are rare, but they are well worth waiting for.

Wild Animals
We Have Known

There is no entry in my journal to tell when the first raccoon discovered our sunken garbage pail, but it was some
time ago. I suppose it was an old patriarch who had
learned what to look for and where. Whether friends followed in his footsteps or whether he passed the information on to his immediate family, I have no way of knowing. Suffice to say, we soon found ourselves playing host
to a number of raccoons of all shapes and sizes.

141

At first we were rather flattered to think that our garbage was sufficiently tempting to attract these midnight visitors. Then we discovered that we were not one of a select few, that we were, in fact, only one stop on a route that included all our neighbors. It was somewhat deflating, in a peculiar sort of way.

We were at a loss to know how they opened that heavy metal cover, and I determined to find out. The garbage pail is only a step from the back porch, so one night I converted the porch into a blind and settled down for a long wait. Actually it was not too long, possibly an hour or so. I saw it coming down the steps from the upper garden, a big coon that sort of flowed over the ground. High living had given it considerable excess weight. It came directly across to the garbage pail, obviously having been there many times before, and approached it from the side where the foot treadle stands up. Pressing the treadle down with its heavy body, it opened the cover wide, then edged around it and reached down inside. It was as simple as that. I should have known that the mastery of such an elementary mechanical detail would pose no problem for an animal as intelligent as a raccoon.

Some of the younger coons did have their problems, not in opening the cover, but in reaching down to their goal. That pail is a foot and a half deep, quite a stretch for a coon which is only half-grown. Hearing a suspicious noise one evening, I went to the kitchen window and flashed a beam out onto the garbage pail. The cover was closed, but sticking out from one side was the end of a raccoon's tail. My immediate thought was that the poor thing was trapped inside, and that I should rush out to its rescue. My concern was short-lived, however, for a moment later the cover began to rise and the coon came backing out. It had been hanging from the rim of the pail by its hind feet, in complete control of the situation.

Frankly these nocturnal visits lost their charm after a short while. The covers were never lowered gently and quietly. Rather, they always went down with a resounding bang, and in the still of the night it was a disconcerting sound, loud enough to wake all but the soundest sleepers. And of course, having been rudely awakened once, we would lie there expecting it to happen again. As often as not the one bang was all, but it had done its job of disturbing a night's sleep. This year has been singularly free of raccoon visitations. There are only two of us at home now, and the volume of garbage has decreased markedly. So has its quality. I cannot imagine that the raccoons find a diet of coffee grounds and grapefruit peels particularly tempting.

The garbage pail is not the only attraction for our black-masked night visitors. One evening I heard a peculiar thumping on the back porch. When I turned on the light I discovered a half-grown coon which had climbed the post to the suet feeder, and it was doing its best to dig out the contents. It was not in the least disturbed by the sudden glare of light. It peered around the post to see what had happened, then returned to its work. I opened the door and went out on the porch. The coon simply edged a bit further around the post, but made no move to leave. Only its hind feet were in view, so I reached out and pinched one gently. At last it got the message, leaped to the ground, and hurried away. The same thing happened the following evening, only this time it was my wife who did the pinching. I wonder how many people have had the experience of pinching the toes of a wild raccoon? We had an explanation of our visitor's behavior a few days later, when a neighbor informed us that Mrs. Shaw had installed floodlights and was feeding numbers of raccoons and skunks each night. No doubt this was one who was accustomed to the bright lights.

Early one morning I saw a raccoon returning from its nightly rounds. It came ambling slowly up the driveway, clambered over the stone wall, and settled itself at the foot of the pine tree, sitting up on its haunches. Here, for some time, it watched the traffic go by. There was very little at that hour, but it certainly seemed interested. We had a pheasant one year who did the same thing. Morning after morning it stood at the top of our upper slope under the bridal-wreath bush and followed the cars going by from right to left, then from left to right. It was rather like watching a spectator at a tennis match. I have seen people sitting in front of their houses doing the same thing as Sunday traffic streams by. I wonder if their thinking is any more involved than that of the coon and the pheasant?

On the trail of the coons came the scavenging skunks. I cannot think there was much left for them that was edible. For a night or two I watched them from my back porch blind, but it was an unrewarding experience. They shuffled around, sniffing and snuffling, then went on their way. This is not to say that skunks are necessarily uninteresting animals. I have made brief mention of Mr. Skunk, our pet in Harvard. We raised him from an infant and kept him all one summer. Our son was then three, and he played with him as he would a kitten, pulling him by the tail, squeezing him tight in affectionate embrace. We even allowed him in the house, at least as far as the kitchen, and although we did not have his scent sacs removed, there was never the slightest odor. In the light of future knowledge, especially about rabies, I am sure I would have been much more cautious, but fortunately all went well. Mr. Skunk was immortalized, in full color against a background of autumnal poison ivy, on a *Natural History* cover.

For a brief period David and I achieved a certain limited fame as skunk removers. It all started one year when I appeared on the program of a book fair along with Thornton Burgess. During the course of our conversation he told me of a unique experience he had had. One evening a neighbor called to say that there was a skunk in his cellar, and since Burgess knew all about animals, would he please come over and remove it. "Well," said Thornton, "I had never done this before, but I'd read about it. Seems the two odor sacs are opened and closed by a bone at the

NATURAL HISTORY

base of the tail. When the tail is down, they're closed off, but when it's raised they're wide open and then look out. So I went over to test the theory, and by golly it worked."

Not long after that conversation I had a similar call from a friend, except that his skunk had fallen into the well outside one of his cellar windows. Figuring if it worked for Thornton Burgess it would work for us, my son and I went out on a relief expedition. The poor beast was pacing back and forth in its narrow confines, and while the entire family watched anxiously from the safety of the house, I lay down on my stomach and reached my hand into the well, slowly, ever so slowly. When the tail came within easy reach, I grabbed and lifted at the same time. My captive never had a chance to raise its tail. It was always in line with the backbone, and although there was a slight odor, there was no real discharge. I carried it to a nearby stone wall and dropped it on the far side. Mission accomplished.

The same thing happened once again, and this time I told my friend that, having seen it done twice, he was now on his own. So he installed screening over all his window wells.

The high spot of our skunk-removal career, however, came when a new school was being built just beyond the ballfield. David, who was self-appointed supervisor of all local construction, came home breathlessly one day with the announcement, "Daddy, we have a job to do. There's a skunk in the Smith School basement." It turned out that the furnace was being installed, but work had been at a standstill for three days because a skunk was wandering about down there.

When we arrived we found the menace was in an ideal situation. It was in a narrow space behind the furnace, a space that was open in both directions. After three days I imagine the skunk was thoroughly frightened and hungry. I gave David his instructions, and while he stood at a safe distance waving his arms and calling to hold the skunk's attention, I edged around the back. Workmen were peering cautiously around corners everywhere as I reached down slowly, then quickly grabbed and lifted. As we walked out with our prize there was no burst of cheering or shouts of joy. I imagine the workmen rather resented seeing an end to their enforced holiday with pay.

One year our woodpile was home for several weeks to a cottontail with very regular habits. Every evening at dusk it emerged to head off somewhere for the night, and every morning in the gray of dawn it returned. The homecoming was no hurried affair. For anywhere up to half an hour it would wander about, nibbling at this and that, standing on its hind legs to get a better view across the way, or just crouching down and resting. Once a pheasant dropped by for a visit. At a distance of no more than three feet they stared at one another. This went on for several minutes, then, finding they had no intelligence to transmit, the pheasant wandered on. Another time a red squir-

rel, in a fit of temper, came charging at the cottontail and chased it off over the hill. I really have no idea whether it was temper or just a game of sorts. In any event they both came back in minutes and from then on paid no attention to one another.

Then came a morning when our rabbit failed to return. I doubt that it had become dissatisfied with our accommodations. I rather fear that, during the course of its nocturnal wanderings, it had run afoul of a hunting fox or an owl. The fact remains, we saw it no more. It is well remembered, however, by innumerable drawings in my sketch book.

A year or so later we had another cottontail in the woodpile, but this was an entirely different type. Its habits were unpredictable and its tenancy of short duration. It is recorded in brief journal entries:

January 1: Another cottontail has taken up residence under our woodpile. It first showed up two days ago, leaving its snug retreat at dusk. It came back yesterday at 8:00 A. M., and left again last evening after a good day's rest. But by 8:15 this morning it had not yet returned, and I have been watching closely. Maybe it's not going to make it today. After all, last night was New Year's Eve, and there were probably some pretty gay rabbit revels going on.

January 9: Those must have been some revels. There has been no sign of our rabbit since New Year's Eve.

February 3: Well, at long last the revels are over. At
2:00 this afternoon our roisterer returned. At least I
assume it's the same one, for after nibbling about a bit
just above the woodpile, it came down directly to the
rabbit hole entrance and went it. This is the second day
of a 50° thaw, and the rain is coming down in torrents.
Whether or not this had anything to do with the return
of the prodigal is open to question, but it's just possible
in such foul weather it may have decided the woodpile
was the dryest possible place to sleep it out.

I have a suspicion that we provide only one of a series
of hideouts, a sort of rabbit motel chain where the days
are spent at the nearest one after a night of wandering.
And maybe ours did not quite come up to the chain's
standards of quality. At least we saw no more of that cottontail after February 3.

Last summer we had our first woodchuck. It appeared
in mid-September, a half-grown youngster, a woodchuck
of the season. At the foot of the steps leading up to the
woodpile there is much more white clover than grass, an
ideal spot for a clover connoisseur. Every morning, as regular as clockwork, it was there nibbling its way through
the clover. As is the custom of woodchucks, it stopped
eating periodically to look around and see that all was
well. At times it would take flight, rushing to the top of
the steps to turn and see whether or not there really was a
menace, or if it was nearer, fleeing to the rock pile behind
the spreading forsythia bush. It was a fat little animal,
evidently ready for a long winter, with light-colored fur

and a dark, almost black cap. About the end of September its morning forays ceased. I was somewhat at a loss to know why. We were having unseasonably warm weather, a real Indian summer that lasted well into October. And the clover was still lush and tempting to one with a taste for that sort of diet.

Hibernation is a subject about which there is still much to learn. Is it triggered by shortening days, by cooler weather, by some internal clockwork? With woodchucks it is undoubtedly the last, for I found a line in a reference book that said: "One of the greatest hibernators of all is the woodchuck. ... It retires to its den in late September or early October, when the weather is still mild and plenty of green food is still growing all about, and sleeps for six months or more." As I write this in January, the ground and the woodpile are deep in snow, and the temperature stands at 2° above zero. That woodchuck is certainly doing something right.

If any of our red squirrels misbehave we have only ourselves to blame, for we introduced them to our yard. It happened one summer when neighbors were about to take off on an extended vacation and were at a loss to know what to do with their pet red squirrel. Would we like to have him? The transfer from their house to ours was quickly made. Our children immediately dubbed him Charlie, after a favorite red-headed character in the comics, Charles C. (for Charles) Charles, of Charles Street, Boston.

Charlie made an attractive pet, was thoroughly photo-

graphed, and as autumn approached he was released at
the foot of the big pine. As we hoped, he climbed up the
trunk, popped into a hole, and took up residence. We
have had red squirrels there ever since, except for three
seasons. The first was when a swarm of bees arrived, and
no one, squirrel or human, argues with several thousand
bees bent on finding a home. The following year the
cavity was probably so crammed with honey combs there
was room for nothing else. Another year, sometime later, a
gray squirrel dispossessed the reds. I wonder where the
present inhabitants come in the line of descent?

Only one of our squirrels has needed disciplining, as
was previously related, and I feel certain it must have
been an interloper, not one of the family. Otherwise it has
been a constant source of pleasure to watch their antics.
They are so alert, attractive, and unpredictable. One may
sit on a limb for a long time, just sunning itself, then suddenly, to paraphrase Stephen Leacock, dash off madly in
all directions. They love a new fall of light snow. They
dive into it with abandon, reappearing some distance
away, alert black eyes peering from faces powdered with
snow as though made up for a stage performance, then
dive back in again.

I do not want to overdo the Thoreauvian quotes, but it
is a great temptation. After all, he was a local boy who
wrote about the same birds and animals who are our
friends, and he was a great nature writer. I shall risk one
more, however, for his description of a red squirrel's antics
is too apt to be overlooked. "All day long the red squirrels

came and went, and afforded me much entertainment by
their maneuvers ... running over the snow crust by fits
and starts like a leaf blown by the wind ... then suddenly
pausing with a ludicrous expression and a gratuitous
somerset, as if all the eyes of the universe were fixed on
him—for all the motions of a squirrel, even in the most sol-
itary recesses of the forest, imply spectators as much as
those of a dancing girl."

Red squirrels have ground-dwelling relatives, chipmunks, and they have always been with us, sometimes in
unwanted numbers. There were two, however, who gave
us a great deal of pleasure. One was Willy, who lived for
several years in the stone wall behind the patio. Willy
became so tame that he would stand on his hind legs and
take sunflower seeds from our hands. It was a most unusual feeling when he rested his little paws on the edge of
our hands and nuzzled around the palm to pick up seeds.
We amused ourselves at times counting the number he
could stuff into his expandable cheek pouches. Thirty-two
was the maximum.

In his first year the patio was all Willy's, but the following season he had competition. We knew where the new
chipmunk came from, a hole in our neighbor's yard. We
would see it pop out, bounce over to the lilacs and, taking
advantage of every bit of cover, come across to join us. If
Willy happened to be there at the time, a fight took place
immediately, a mad whirlwind chase under the chairs,
through the garden, over our feet, until one finally left the
scene temporarily. At first the interloper was the aggres-

sor (we could tell the difference because Willy had only half a tail), so it acquired an obvious name, Nemesis. But at last Willy began to stand up for his rights—after all, it was his patio. We enjoyed those two, as did our guests who had never hand-fed a wild animal before. Unfortunately both were victims of the tomato-eating episode and were transported elsewhere. Willy's bobtail was no help in identification since this is a common condition among chipmunks, probably because of all that fighting—as much of a hallmark as broken noses among human fighters.

At one point I needed a close-up photograph of a chipmunk, so I laid out food on a flat stone projecting from the sloping end wall of the patio. It was almost guaranteed to be a successful venture; and, indeed, it was. I discovered, however, that there was competition for the food. Every now and then a shrew would dart out from a recess behind the stone, snatch up a seed, and dash back in again. So I got shrew photographs as well. A shrew's eyesight is not of the best. Spending all its life in dark tunnels, it has little need for seeing. In one of its headlong dashes this shrew overshot the mark and fell over the edge to the hard bricks below. A drop of two feet or more is quite a shock to a shrew. For a moment or two it lay there, legs spread wide, then gathered itself together and rushed off as though nothing unusual had happened. A shrew has a small body but a tremendous amount of nervous energy. It was the latter that won out.

If the title of this chapter has a familiar ring to older

readers, that is the intent. After *Two Little Savages*, my
favorite Ernest Thompson Seton book as a boy was *Wild
Animals I Have Known.* Our acquaintances are not too
different from his. He wrote of Silverspot, the crow, Rag-
gylug, the cottontail rabbit, and Redruff, the partridge.
His stories are much more complete, much more dramatic
than the bits and pieces I have recorded here. But I feel
sure we have been just as interested in and have had just
as much pleasure from our wild friends as he did. I, therefore, have no hesitancy at all about lifting his title, almost
intact, for this chapter.

A Basis for Miracles

As I reread these pages I am astonished at how many things I had originally planned to include that have been omitted. There is no mention, for example, of my wife's frequent trips to the meat counter of our local market and, while other customers stared in disbelief, blandly asked the meat man, "Bill, do you have any chicken heads for me today?" That was the summer we were raising a great horned owl. There has been only brief reference to Mr. Crow, one of our liveliest and most exasperating pets,

157

who roamed about at will. He delighted in pulling clothespins off the line and stuffing them in the down-spouts of the roof gutters, while our clothes blew about the countryside.

I have not even mentioned the gall insects about which so little is known, and of which we have a great number. Some go so far as to change their shapes and habits from one year to another. Nor have I written of the parasitic ichneumon "wasps," especially the big Thalessa whose long, fragile-appearing ovipositor drills deep into live wood to lay an egg in the tunnel of wood-boring sawfly larvae. We have had these, too. There was no place to tell of the tiny red pseudo-scorpions who hitchike rides on the legs of flies, two of which I found on a dead fly clinging to one of our kitchen windows.

The big white-faced hornets who built their nest on one of our back-hill sugar maples is a story in itself. In fact it became one with the title, *The Tale of the White-Faced Hornet*. I should like to have told of the mud-dauber wasps who somehow manage to get into our attic each summer and plaster their spider-filled nurseries on the sides of our chimney. There are so many other creatures and happenings that have been of real interest to us, but, unfortunately, if a book is not to become encyclopedic, the line must be drawn somewhere.

If these pages open the eyes of even a few readers to the great variety of life in their own back yards, then this book will have fulfilled its purpose. With that awakened interest will come a new understanding and awareness, a sympathy for the natural world, a care for nature. This is the basis, the very foundation upon which depend many cures for the environmental ills that beset us. When that sympathy becomes widespread, miracles can be accomplished.